Wherever

God

Takes Me

a memoir by

Senol Kiane

Open Books Press
Bloomington, Indiana

Published by Open Books Press, USA

www.OpenBooksPress.com
info@OpenBooksPress.com

An imprint of Pen & Publish, Inc.
www.PenandPublish.com
Bloomington, Indiana
(314) 827-6567

Print ISBN: 978-1-941799-44-4
eBook ISBN: 978-1-941799-45-1

Library of Congress Control Number: 2016920256

Printed on acid-free paper.

What God Plans

We make plans, unaware of what is being planned,
and what we plan cannot withstand what God plans.

The servant deliberates, and to him it seems so clear.
Yet though he plays his tricks, he can't play God.

If a good-hearted man takes a couple of steps forward,
then who knows where God will take him?

— Jalāl ad-Dīn Muhammad Rūmī

Introduction

I met Senol Kiane in March 1998. We had both been married before. From very early on, we knew we wanted to spend our lives together. We just fit.

I felt there was something special about Senol. When I looked into his eyes, I could feel something much more to him. I think because of our connection, he felt that he could trust me. With that, he began to tell me about his earlier experiences, right up to things happening to him while we were together. (In those days, his guardian angel, Isaac, was speaking directly to him, and not through him, so this was not documented.)

I was amazed. I wanted to know everything. I would bombard him with questions. I couldn't get enough. I believed him with every fiber of my body.

Early in 2001, we were told that my father was dying of heart failure. Senol suggested we bring our wedding plans forward so my dad could see us get married. Thankfully, he did. We married in February 2001; my Dad passed away two months later. He was just fifty-three years old.

At this time, Senol's experiences began to increase. I was hungry for them, because I wanted that connection with my dad beyond this life.

However, my grief was multiplied tenfold when, eight months after my dad passed, my brother, friend, and soulmate Behcet died suddenly two days before Christmas at age thirty-one. He'd been shopping for presents. I was inconsolable. If it wasn't for Senol and his spiritual knowledge and guidance, I wouldn't be who I am today. Thanks to him, I have accounts of my brother's and father's lives, their duties, messages, and so on.

Everything changed for Senol after Behcet's passing, too. His experiences changed. The first time I saw this, I thought he was having a heart attack. It was the first time somebody spoke through him to relay a message. This was my brother. When my shock of witnessing this died down, I documented it. This would be the beginning of my documentation; if you could see how his experiences have evolved, you would be amazed.

I believe with all my heart that God put him in my life for a reason greater than anything I can explain through writing.

It's a reason I can only reach in my deepest soul, beyond the limitations of words. I thank God for him every day, for I know that I share my life with a living miracle. I take what I have learned to comfort others who are going through life's struggles, which gives them comfort.

Senol is not a healer, medium, or psychic. He certainly does not proclaim himself to be anything like it, which, to me, speaks to how genuine he is. He cannot be categorized, in my opinion, because he comprises all of these things and so much more.

One part of him lives with me, and with us, on the earthly plane. The other lives on the heavenly plane. I am the fortunate person who experiences this with him every day. Now, we share some of these experiences with you.

—Aycan Kiane

Note from the Author

I carry the power of love and answers to the question of how people might live well in this life. All of us would see past the way we think if we opened our hearts. Every day, I feel the pain that each person experiences. I can feel their sorrow and happiness and I can sometimes hear their pain. They ask God, "Why me?" "Why can things not go right for me in my life?" "Why did my mother, father, sister, brother, child die?" "Why can I not hold down a job?" "Why did I lose my home or business?"

The questions are endless. What I will reveal and share with you will not only serve to answer your questions, but also open your hearts. I will tell you how God touched me when things looked bleak. I can show you that life is not just here and now; when we die, life continues. We are part of a circle of life. Our life has been set in its higher intentions since the time before we were born.

No matter what religious background or where in the world we are from, we are all created the same. From the moment we take our first steps and progress to awareness of all five senses, we can distinguish right from wrong.

However, we have somehow lost our way and lost sight of the true path.

We need to look inside ourselves—the only way to start healing each and every person. Then and only then can we really change the world—but how? First, we must have faith and belief in God, and then understand there is a heaven and hell. Some say heaven and hell are right here on earth. That might be right in our physical sense, because we all experience good and bad things in life. When we feel despair, sadness, or sorrow, it may seem that we are in hell. When we feel joy and happiness and things are going right, perhaps we feel heaven on earth.

How do I know heaven and hell exist and are real? Because I have been blessed by God with a gift that has allowed me to visit both places.

Our endless pursuit of what we believe is happiness sometimes results in decisions we may later regret. The choices we make in order to achieve that happiness always have consequences, good and bad. I aim to show from my own spiritual experiences that we can grow and be better. True happiness is there for all of us, should we choose to open our hearts. However, most of us are blind. Think of what we are blinding ourselves from: our hearts are not just sources of life, but keys to true happiness. We put limits on ourselves. Why? Because we are human and have been conditioned in this way. For the few of us who can see beyond this conditioning, we know there is so much more. My aim is to show you the truth.

Together, let us take this wonderful journey to the truth. I will show you that the body we have been blessed with is just a vessel, a form of visitation into this wonderful world that God has created. When our time in this body is over and we are laid to rest, our real life will begin, one in which time ceases to exist.

—Senol Kiane
North London, England
2016

Chapter One

To let go of fear is to have no ego.
To let go of fear is to have love.
To let go of fear is to have light.
To let go of fear is to have compassion.
To let go of fear is a means to help others.
To let go of fear is to have heart.
To let go of fear is a means to a true awakening.
Let God and the light always guide you.

When I was six, I was playing alone with my favorite red ball in my bedroom, but I was not alone. I realized there were other children playing beside me. They were happy, smiling children, with a beautiful light emanating from them, but they were not of this world. Then I then noticed a taller, older figure standing in the corner, smiling and watching over us. His light was even brighter than the children's. He was there for a reason other than to watch over us, but I knew that I was safe and that I could trust him. I felt just as safe with him, if not safer, than I did with my own parents.

I approached him. He knelt down to my level, and I asked, "Who are you? What is your name?"

"My name is Isaac." Before I could tell him my name, he added, "I know who you are. Your name is Senol."

I was surprised and excited. "Who told you? How do you know my name?"

Isaac said that he knew my name from the time before I was born. He also told me why I received my name: for a very powerful reason, for its specific meaning: "Senol" means "life." He then proceeded to tell me that he would reveal more when I came of age, and that he would always be by my side to guide and protect me. He said that I had been given a beautiful gift, and he would unveil that gift when the time was right.

I thought that I would finally be given the object of my dreams: a shiny new bike. Little did I know. It was almost as if he knew my inner thoughts and chuckled when this thought crossed my mind.

Before he left, Isaac turned to me and said, "They will know when they look into your eyes that you are an angel and that you are full of love and compassion. They will be drawn to you."

He gathered the other children in the room and walked into a huge bright light that appeared from nowhere. A moment later, they were gone. I was again alone in my bedroom, very sad and lonely. However, this miraculous event would be the first of many more to come. As I grew older, I began to realize I was different. I was given signs in some form or another to forewarn me of something bad happening. Maybe it had just happened, like a death in the family or a serious illness. A message passed on by an angel to warn me. If we visited family or friends, I could sense it if there was a negative or positive energy in the home and around the people who lived there.

It felt strange. I could not name it, as I did not know what I was feeling and why.

I could not tell anyone in my family about this. What would I say? If I spoke, they would tell me it was my imagination or that I was being silly.

I decided to ignore it all. I did not want to see or hear the angels or the messages I received. I wanted to be as normal as any other teenage boy. I wanted to play football with my friends. I wanted to date girls. I wanted a normal life.

Then one day, when I was seventeen and walking to college, I suddenly felt completely detached from my body. It was almost as if I were in a bubble. Silence surrounded me. I thought I was coming down with the flu. I knew the direction I was heading, but I was not paying any attention to my surroundings. I felt cut off. I came to an intersection, and without looking left or right I just continued walking. Then something extraordinary happened. In a split second, I was looking down upon myself crossing the road, completely oblivious to oncoming traffic; the scene unfolding in slow motion, like a dream. I saw a fast-approaching white van. I could not avert it nor warn myself. In a split second just before impact, I slowly turned and put my right hand out toward the vehicle. I felt the impact of the van hitting my hand; it came to a dead stop.

I continued to walk across to the other side of the road, the moment continuing to open in slow motion. I looked back. The driver gazed at me in shock, mouth agape, whilst checking the vehicle for damage. There was none.

I found myself back in my body and continued on my way, not giving it another thought. At least not for a few years. Although I continued to experience spiritual phenomena through my early adulthood, I chose to ignore it. The angels would appear in front of me and I would just walk past them. I could hear them say, "Senol, you have to embrace the gift that has been given to you. You cannot continue to ignore us."

My automatic response: "Leave me alone. Why do you continue to follow me? Who am I to have been chosen—chosen to do what?"

"When you stop fighting this, we will reveal to you why," they said.

To others, it may have seemed as though I were talking to myself, but they were real, standing in front of me, as clear as the next person in the room. I could see them and hear them, but still I continued to fight and tried to live my life normally.

Then one day, when I was twenty, I was jogging home after training. I was an amateur boxer in a club not far from home. Boxing was my life, my release, the only thing in my life I could control. I threw myself into it and grew skillful.

Very skillful. My dream was to become a professional boxer. On this day, out of nowhere, an angel appeared in front of me. It happened so quickly that I came to a dead stop. The angel asked, "Do you want to see why?"

"What is it you want to show me?" I replied.

He told me to turn and look ahead. . . . All of a sudden, I found myself in a different dimension, no longer on earth. My physical self stayed in place, but my consciousness did not.

"Am I in heaven?" I asked.

"Yes." He held both his hands out toward me, but I realized he was not offering them for me to hold, but directing my attention to what was happening on earth: war and famine, people suffering, pain and sorrow, such sadness.

Overwhelming sadness. "What can I do? I have no part in this; it is not my doing. What do you want from me?" I asked.

"You have been given a gift, the ability to speak the words of love, peace, and compassion. Once you embrace this, you will be able to help and save many. Through your words, you will touch many souls, but before you begin your journey, before you accept your gift, you have to fight and defeat your demons."

Before I could ask him what he meant, a very powerful energy wrapped around me with thundering force. In a split second, I returned to the spot in which I'd been standing, breathless and disorientated. My body trembled. Still in shock, I began to walk slowly, then my pace quickened into a jog, then a run. I wanted to get home as fast as possible to try to make sense of what had happened.

Years later, I realized something: this message of fighting my demons was delivered because, until I did fight them, I would not encounter any angels again. I had to overcome my fears and doubts . . . even my faith.

I had no one to turn to. I was afraid and confused. I was not ready to face it alone. I kept telling myself that nobody would believe me. They would think I was mad and probably lock me away. The best thing I could do? Put this away and continue to live with some sense of normality.

That is exactly what I did. Three years later, I got married. My wife and I bought a house in Essex and settled down. We had two beautiful children who brought such joy and happiness into my life, and I threw myself into being the best father I could be. I never revealed any of these experiences to my wife or children. I did not think that my wife would understand. After thirteen years of marriage, we drifted apart and decided to divorce.

A very dark period followed. My children were everything to me, and I could not imagine being away from them. When the time came to take them back home to their mum, I returned to my one-bedroom apartment feeling a huge emptiness. I felt as though my life were not worth living. My cousins did their best to help and comfort me and tried to brighten my outlook. They were all I had, as my immediate family was completely unaware of my situation. Just what I wanted.

However, the despair of handing my children back, not being with them or there for them all the time, was creating a devastating effect on me. I had never felt so alone. I decided my life was not worth living. I attempted suicide by taking tablets, but I did not really want to die. I wanted to cry. For help.

I managed to call my cousin. He rushed immediately to my side and took me to the hospital. They pumped my stomach and gave me a life-saving lecture about how painful, slow, and agonizing overdosing on tablets would make my death.

This was the wake-up call I needed. The hospital put me in touch with a therapist, and slowly, I began to put my life back together. There were days when I sat alone in my apartment and grew very depressed. I broke down crying and held my head in my hands, questioning, *Why is this happening to me?*

One time, a voice spoke: "You are not alone. You have to go through this in order to be cleansed."

A moment of clarity followed. I remembered my last revelation and recognized my struggles as the demons I had to overcome.

After completing therapy, I decided to move back to my parents' house. I explained what had happened to me and they were very saddened. I resumed work and began to rebuild my life.

Living with my parents became a colorful adventure within itself. They are stubborn and old fashioned. My parents emigrated from Northern Cyprus in the late fifties and came from a very humble background. Since I was born and bred in England, I had very different views and ideas. I'm still fighting this battle today. For example, one day, when the post arrived, it contained a telephone bill, among other things. When my father looked at the bill, shock overtook him. "Who has been using my phone? This is an outrage." He turned to me. "Look at this!"

I had to hold back my laughter. The outrageous bill was £34.00 (less than $50). Inexpensive. I tried to tell him this, but he would not listen. He accused me of overusing his telephone. Apparently, each time he walked into the room, I would be on the telephone; from that, he deduced it must be me. I told him that I only answered when the phone rang, and there is no charge for incoming calls. He didn't accept my explanation, because all he could see was me on the phone. I found myself with my hand on my temple: the beginning of a migraine. Rather than continue this conversation, I decided to pay the bill and recognized that this was a test of my patience.

Chapter Two

Instead of saying "I wish I were part of it," be a part of it.
Come forward and say, "Yes, I want to make it happen."
Anything is possible.

Through mutual friends, I met the woman who would become my wife. Although we met when I was still experiencing inner turmoil about the path my life was taking, I realized that this girl, Aycan, had come when I needed stability and new direction. For me, it was love at first sight.

For her, it was not. Something to do with the color of my trousers did not bode well, apparently. However, she later told me, my eyes saved the day, for which I am very grateful. At first, the impact we would make on each others' lives did not occur to us. We had both been married before, and although she did not have children, I knew she was the right person to whom I could introduce my children. She had so much love to give. Her outlook and positivity slowly caused me to realize that I still had a chance of a happy life. She nurtured me.

Even though it was a struggle at first, since I felt unworthy of being loved, she persevered. We began living together and I finally started to settle down.

During Christmas 2000, Aycan's father became seriously ill with heart disease. He had been struggling with this for some years, but now we all knew that time was running out. He spent more and more time in the hospital; he deteriorated rapidly. Aycan and I decided in February 2001 to get married so he could watch us exchange vows before he passed. We planned the wedding in three days. Between the quick planning and the number of guests—only 240 compared to the average 500-person Mediterranean wedding—I think we must have broken a world record. The day went by beautifully, and my father-in-law was very happy. Two months later, he passed away.

Aycan is extremely close to her family and enjoyed a close bond with her father. Her relationship with her brother, Behcet, was also very strong. Although she struggled with this loss, it affected her brother even more. His worsening condition worried us. We could all see that he was not coping well. He could not understand how he could lose his father at such a young age, him being thirty, his father fifty-three. Their father-son bond grew more special when Behcet had become a father himself. Behcet was looking forward to receiving fatherly advice on how to be as good as his father was to him.

Before the time of my father-in-law's death, I was still ignoring my spiritual side and messages, living my life as normally as one can.

When he died, a light switched on. Everything started flooding through and I could not stop it. Little did I know that this would be the beginning of a path where I had to relinquish all control. I thought I was in control, never considering my deeper gift would catch up with me. *It was something I would grow out of,* I thought. Like having a common cold: ignore it and it would go away. But it was not to be. Not only had the gift come back, but now, it was stronger than ever. My spiritual experiences were occurring more and more often.

When I first met Aycan, I told her about my childhood but skimmed over certain other times in my life. I was testing her reaction. To my amazement, she was fascinated and asked so many questions I could not keep up with the answers. She did not think me mad. On the contrary, as she now says, she recognized I was special and had a gift. It also confirmed to her that God places people in others' lives for a reason. He always has a plan, a fact we should never question.

Nothing could have prepared us for what happened eight months after my father-in-law passed away. Two days before Christmas, we arranged to meet Aycan's brother, his wife, and twenty-two-month-old son to do some Christmas shopping. We took a break for lunch; the place was packed full of people with the same intention.

I had noticed Behcet was looking agitated and irritable. Aycan put this down to holiday stress and the sheer volume of people. This did not sit right with me, and I kept watching him, reading him at this point. He ordered his favorite meal, burger and fries. He took a very small bite of his burger and two fries and left the rest. He said he was full. We were shocked. This never happened. I did not say anything else about it to Aycan, as I knew how worried she could get, especially regarding her brother. I could see two angels standing on either side of him.

I decided to keep this to myself, praying that I was wrong. *I did not just see that. Not possible.* We all said our goodbyes and arranged to go to her family's house later that night for a visit.

Half an hour later, we arrived home and had just made a cup of tea when the telephone rang. I answered it. All I could hear was screaming: Aycan's sister-in-law. She could tell me only that Behcet had collapsed. I kept asking her where the rest of the family was. They were still at the shopping mall. "We're on our way," I said.

I turned to my wife. "We have to return to the mall. Your brother has collapsed," I said softly.

She became hysterical, more so because she believed I knew something and was not telling her. My face said it all, but I tried to console her by telling her not to worry. By the time we arrived, emergency services was on the scene and the paramedics worked on him. We were not allowed near him. They carried him into the ambulance, and the police escorted us to the hospital. No one told us he passed away on arrival, but I knew.

On the way to the hospital, I managed to contact other members of Aycan's family and was relieved to see some of them upon our arrival. They had done everything they could to revive him, but he could not be saved. They wheeled him into a quiet room. Only family members were allowed in. At first, Aycan said she wanted to see him, but she was too distraught. It had taken all my will to calm her down. She then decided that she could not see him lifeless in a cold hospital room. I asked family members to stay with her while I walked in alone to see him.

I looked down and held his hand. It was still warm. Suddenly, I saw him standing in the corner of the room, looking at me. "Behcet," I said, "you are lying here. I am holding your hand. You're dead."

He smiled. *"I am only dead in body. You did the right thing by not letting her come in to see me lying here; she would not have been able to handle it."*

He asked me to tell Aycan and her mum that he loved them very much. He wanted his wife and son to know how much he loved them, too. *"I am home now, with dad,"* he said. He added that he felt no pain when he passed. *"I have something else to tell you, Senol. God has given you a gift. Stop running from it. He expects great things from you because your time has come."*

I gave him my love and said goodbye. There was no more turning back from what was expected of me.

Now was not the right time to reveal what had just occurred. My main task was to help my wife and her family get through this devastating event. I was afraid for her because she looked very vulnerable. She was not coping well at all. I thought she might even harm herself. Since it was two days before Christmas, arranging the funeral was very difficult. Everything was shut down over the holidays. It took almost two weeks before Behcet was finally laid to rest.

During this time of waiting, the most moving thing came one day when my wife was looking out the window, watching people walk by.

"Up until now, my life was going in one direction," she said. "Now that he is gone, I feel my life has gone too. These people who are walking by are getting on with their lives totally unaware that mine will never be the same again."

"This is the circle of life," I said softly. "You grieve but you have to carry on. This is what is expected. God does not give more than we can handle."

I continued sharing. The power of losing someone you love so much is such a mighty energy that when God created us in human form, he gave us the ability to carry on, even though we suffered mighty loss. "Everyone loses someone, you have to look outside and see," I added. "These people you see walking by have experienced loss but they carry on. You may not see it right now, because you cannot see through your pain, but you will, as time goes on. I promise you that."

A year later, as we approached the first anniversary of my brother-in-law's passing, I found myself analyzing all the experiences since, especially when he spoke to me straight after his passing. I remembered him telling me that I had a wonderful gift and that I should stop running from it. I still was not sure what I was meant to do, but I knew that it was important. God was expecting me to step up. But step up to what? That was what I was trying to work out.

Meanwhile, unbeknownst to me, my wife had visited a clairvoyant that same day. She wanted to make contact with her father and brother. She did not tell me because she knew that I was struggling spiritually and she did not want to add to this. She also was afraid of my disapproval. During her visit, her father came to her and gave her a message, and then she waited for the medium woman to continue about her brother. He did not come. She asked the clairvoyant about it, but she could only get a message from her dad.

My wife left and came home. She looked upset, but I did not push her. She was very quiet, so I tried to lighten the mood. We made ourselves comfortable in the front room and put on a movie. Halfway through, I noticed a very bright light shining powerfully through the opposite window. I tried to ignore it and continue to watch the movie, but noticed it was getting stronger and stronger and coming toward me. As I turned and looked directly at the light, I saw a figure. Looking closer, I recognized this person. "Oh my God. It's your brother!" I shouted.

He continued coming toward me and entered my body. I fell back with immense force. My entire being went into shock. I was shaking and sweating, and found myself no longer in my body. I looked down, watching my wife on the floor crying, thinking that I was suffering a heart attack. I could see her reach for the telephone to call for help.

It was then that her brother spoke through me and called her name. She froze. It was not my voice, but her brother's. When she looked at my face, she did not see me. She saw him. He told her that he wanted to come to her and tell her that he was fine, he was happy and in a beautiful place with their dad and other family members. He passed on his love and withdrew. When he departed, I found myself back in my body, completely drained of energy, as if I had run a marathon.

Although I could remember looking down, I did not carry a complete memory of what had taken place. Aycan, in shock herself, had to find the strength to tell me everything that had happened. She now knew that she had a link or contact to her father and brother through me. This gave her comfort and helped her understand so much more. It was then that she told me about her visit to the clairvoyant. As she did, all the pieces came together: her brother wanted me to pass messages to her. From that moment on, everything changed, and I truly understood that my life would never be the same again.

Chapter Three

Acknowledgment is divine.
Acceptance is divine.
Belief is divine.
Embracing truth is divine.

I **wanted answers. I finally accepted that I had to walk** the spiritual path, but I did not know where to go. Whom could I speak to? Who could tell me what was happening to me?

My friend Huseyin is extremely spiritual—a man I trust completely. He never ridiculed me, but instead listened and guided me to the correct path. I called and explained to him briefly what had happened, and he came to visit me. When we sat down, I told him everything, from my first childhood experiences to the last with my brother-in-law.

"Can you feel people's emotions and at times read them as well?" he asked. "Have you come across any angels or guardian angels in your home or in other people's homes? Do you hear the sounds of angels?"

"Yes," I answered to all of these questions. "I see, feel, hear, smell, and sense them."

He looked at me quietly, almost in awe. He asked if he could test me. I was relieved that he believed me and curious about the test. Did he know something I did not?

He took out a photo album from his bag and placed it on my lap. Inside were photos from spiritual and holy places that he had visited all around the world.

Then it happened: I fell into a trance, my eyes closed, my face turned away, my right hand hovering above the album. He asked me to name the spiritual site on the first page. I told him what it was, where it was, and described its spiritual significance. Each time he turned the page, I similarly identified each new picture. Heat radiated from my hand as it hovered over every major location. I had never been to any of these places, but they all felt familiar to me.

Huseyin could not believe what he was seeing. My head was still turned and my eyes closed. He closed the book and told me to take my hand away. As I did so, I slowly came back to myself.

I opened my eyes and looked at him. I was very emotional and so was he. He said, "Senol, do you feel that you have so much to share that it becomes overwhelming for you?"

"Yes. I feel as if I am a giant well overflowing with words that I have to convey but do not know where to start. I also feel as though my body does not feel like my own anymore; I look at my hands and do not recognize them. I look into my eyes in the mirror and do not recognize them. I feel very overwhelmed by it all. I know you are going to find this strange, but I can feel the pain of the earth. I feel the pain that people inflict on each other, especially when children are hurt. I find it very hard to control my emotions. I feel as if a volcano is waiting to erupt inside of me. I want to scream at the top of my voice to stop the abuse that we are inflicting on each other and especially the earth.

"I also hear a voice that speaks to me very clearly above the rest saying, 'My son, I will reveal myself to you and when I do you will know me. It is then that your work will begin.'"

I paused and looked at my friend, then added that I hear this voice constantly and it gets stronger as time goes on. Looking steadily back at me, he said, "You have been chosen, Senol. God chooses people every now and again to do his work and he wants you to do his work. When you do, you will meet others who have been chosen, too."

I felt very relieved to share this with somebody I trusted. Even more importantly, he believed what I was telling him. It was not a secret any longer. He told me how happy this made him because he had always known that there was something special about me. He asked me if it was okay for him to do an astrology reading of my birth. I agreed.

He took all the information that he needed, including the date and time of my birth, and began the reading. Shock began to register on his face. He could hardly speak, unsure whether he should reveal most of the reading, as it was almost certainly a divine secret. The only thing he could manage to tell me was that I was a very holy person who had been chosen by God to give love to humanity. He could see that I would be traveling across the world to share the words that God wanted me to reveal. "Many people will want to come and see you, to hear you speak," he added.

I was shocked, but somehow I had already known that he was going to reveal this. My question: how should I begin? All I knew for certain was that Huseyin would play a significant role in my life spiritually.

Soon, people began to hear about me through word of mouth. They would ask me questions about heaven and what it was like, and I would begin to explain in great detail. Then they would ask me if I could make contact with their loved ones who had passed. I tried to explain that I was not a medium, that although I had contact with the other side, I could not switch it on and off at will like a light switch. I explained that it was only possible if their loved ones had something to pass on, that only then would it happen—and without warning.

Up until this point, the only person who had experienced this was Aycan. At first, I was not in control of my body or senses. It might look to anyone as if I were having a stroke or a heart attack. My whole body would convulse, and I would leave my body as the person who has passed entered it and spoke directly to their loved ones. I would return completely drained, and it would take me some time to get back to normal. There were times I could not recall what had just happened. Often I found myself in situations where people would be very insistent, wanting my help to make contact with their loved ones. I would try to explain that there was no guarantee that contact could be made. I knew through my experiences that when a person greatly desires something like this, they can unknowingly put a block on it spiritually. It became difficult, because I never wanted to disappoint.

The first time I had an out-of-body experience with someone other than my wife was quite a shock for those who witnessed it. Two family members had requested to see me, a brother and sister who had just lost their father very recently. They were still grieving. "Okay, but it may be too soon," I said. I knew nothing more about this brother and sister or the deceased.

When they arrived, they sat in front of me. I told them not to expect too much, as their father may not be ready. The girl took out her mobile phone and handed it to me. I looked at a picture of her father's dead body on the screen, just before he was going to be laid to rest.

Within seconds, I went into shock. The mobile flew out of my hand and I went into a trance. I immediately left my body and found myself watching angels with a beautiful white light emanating from all of them. They surrounded the deceased man, now on his knees with arms stretched out, held by the angels who were cleansing his spirit with divine water. The water glittered, water unlike any kind we know here. The man looked at me and smiled. I said, "Forgive me for entering while you are being prepared." He kept smiling until an angel spoke to me and asked, "What is it you wish to ask, divine son?"

"I wish for something that I can pass on to the man's son and daughter, an acknowledgment from him," I replied.

It seemed the man had a unique way of kissing and hugging his daughter. He would kiss her on the forehead for comfort and hold her in a certain way. The angel told me, showed how it was done . . . and then I found myself back in my body, in the room.

The man's son and daughter sobbed hysterically. I thought that I had done something wrong, but instead the woman hugged and thanked me. She knew that she had made contact with her father because, through me, he kissed and hugged her in their special way. She had no doubt that this was her father. She was overjoyed. "That was my dad. I could feel him and smell him when he kissed and hugged me!"

"I'm happy that I could do this for you," I said.

Afterward, I threw myself into meditation. I wanted to learn all I could about my gift, how to balance myself and find some inner peace in order to strengthen myself to help others. I knew also that I had the gift of healing. I began visiting a local shop that specialized in all things spiritual and paranormal.

One day, I started talking with the owner, who had noticed me. I explained a little bit about myself. Fascinated, he directed me toward the correct scent of incense sticks and candles, healing crystals, and meditation CDs. He wanted my contact details because he said he had a lot of clients would be interested in contacting me.

Not long after, I received a phone call from an African lady who had picked up my card from the shop and been referred by the owner. She asked if I could see her immediately. "Why?" I wondered. In a panicked and fearful voice, she said she could not explain on the phone, but must speak to me in person. We agreed on a time and day for me to meet her at her home in East London.

Aycan came with me to create a more comfortable atmosphere for the lady, who was very well spoken and polite. When I suggested we go somewhere private where we could speak, she took me to her lounge. "We must not be disturbed until we are finished speaking," I said. Aycan remained in the kitchen with another woman, the African lady's friend.

My host explained why she had called me there and what she wanted me to do. She was aware of my being a healer and explained what was happening to her. "Every night," she said, "I am visited by a dark, sinister spirit that is very frightening." She would be in her bed, not yet asleep, and it would come to her and abuse her in indescribable ways.

It was draining her of her energy, causing great distress and affecting the quality of her life. She had tried to seek help, but every time somebody tried to intervene, it angered the dark spirit even more and made matters worse. The abuse was escalating and she wanted to put an end to it so that she could live a normal life. "Can you help me?" she asked.

"Yes, of course." I noticed crosses on the wall so I assumed that she believed in God. I began to explain to her the process of cleansing. "You will feel all sorts of emotions and physical sensations, and that they may not feel good. Do not break contact with me once I begin, no matter how strong the feeling. You must be strong."

I lit some incense and put on a CD of prayers. I knew these prayers would help remove any dark spirits or demons that were around. I asked her to lay on the sofa and placed my right hand on her heart and left hand on my own heart.

We both fell into an altered state of consciousness . . . and found ourselves in a very dark place. I told her not to be afraid, that I would not let anything happen to her, that I would be with her the whole way through.

Her body began to convulse. She made very strange noises. A dark spirit began to scream at me, asking me to stop. The sound emanated from the woman, though it was no longer her voice. I prayed relentlessly, holding her hand until finally she jumped into the light with me. *Safe.*

Back in our bodies, we watched the dark spirit rise from her, sucked away into what I can only describe as a black hole that swallowed it up and closed. The woman broke down and cried. She felt free, she said, and knew that it was gone. She felt almost reborn. She could not stop thanking me. For the next year, she called with updates and news about her life. Last I heard, she met a nice man and was to be engaged. She was very happy.

Chapter Four

From where there is darkness,
there will always be light.
From where there is doubt,
there will always be hope.

While relaxing at home on an October day in 2005, I had an out-of-body experience. I knew that this one was going to be different. The sensation felt different. I was being taken somewhere. Before leaving completely, I told Aycan, "You need to write this down." I knew it needed to be documented.

I was gone for about fifteen minutes. When I returned, I remembered everything in clear detail. It was the first time I had experienced such clarity after leaving and returning:

> *I stand on pure white sand, very hot. "There are rocks," my friend Huseyin says while following me. "Do you want me to come with you?"*
> *"Yes."*

> *Hundreds of people walk down a hill and congregate at the bottom, looking at me. They walk around me and start bowing; I take my shoes off. Huseyin has to take his off, too. They watch Huseyin and I climb up the hill. As we reach the top, trumpets blow. We both fall to our knees. A very bright white light appears, and a voice asks me to come forward to receive words: "You have to help end pain and suffering in the world. Huseyin will bear witness to this event. He will log and write everything. Everything will be revealed, spoken through you. You are ready. It has begun."*

From that point on, we wrote down everything—date, time of event, the duration of the experience. These visions were not just spiritual experiences, but carried deeper meaning.

Each time I went back and read over what was written, I knew that I was moving toward something bigger. I was not sure when the next vision would come. I was constantly surrounded by the sounds of heaven, angels singing, and beautiful prayers.

Even though this was becoming continuous, I had to carry on with normality. The strange thing was that, while living this so-called normal life in the outside world, a rebirth was occurring inside. I began to remember what my guardian had said to me when I was a child: all the questions could be answered by him. I had always seen myself traveling the world meeting people, speaking with them, and helping them. This idea was not strange; I felt as if I had done it before. Now these images were coming strong and fast, as though a piece of film was being constantly replayed, people listening to me speak while I gave them words coming to me of divine inspiration. These words touched them, moved them to tears. They made sense. They told me they wanted to feel God and make a spiritual connection with Him in the way that I do.

On May 4, 2006, at 10:30 p.m., I had another experience, recorded as follows:

The whole world is in my hands. I am surrounded by children and adults dressed in pure white. I say to them that I am not ready, that this is too much responsibility. I am then told by the Divine that strength has been given to my hands. "The journey is not complete. As you near you will receive more strength. So much has been done and so much has been forgotten. So much has the world left behind. As the tears of the innocent go unheard I feel them suffering. Forgiveness is something that has been taken for granted. I have given them a choice. We cannot interfere. I have given thee the heart and the mind. I have given thee knowledge of right and wrong. And yet so many ask, "Why?" The answer is there in their hearts. If they search their hearts they will find the answer. To worship. To pray. To love one another.

"You take these things and you use them for wrong. Perfection is in the heart; when the soul is free you

will see perfection. I made you all to see what you may achieve and yet you have lost so much. I have sent so many in the past to give you words of guidance and love. Yet you chose to misunderstand and misread the words. Words that were meant to be pure, you changed. Twisted to suit your ego for your own selfish gain. Suffering and pain were endured by my chosen ones to no avail. So for this I have given mankind free will. Atonement is there. It will always be there for those who wish to be atoned. The heart is the soul of the spiritual light. Everything comes from the heart. It pumps life into the body and it continues after the body has gone. This I reveal, for it is a question many of you ask. Peace be upon all my children. I have not forgotten you. I will always smile on all my children. For the heart will always remain. The heart is cleansed even as it is leaving the body."

When I returned to my body, I was exhausted and shocked. The Divine had spoken directly. My wife was astonished. She told me that a light emanated from me. It lasted for some time.

From that moment on, I began to experience the world very differently. I was becoming part of everything. I was feeling the vibrations of the earth. If I touched a rock, I could feel it resonate. If I touched grass, I could feel its energy. If I touched a tree, I could feel its life force. Everything around me had a different sound. A different feeling. I realized that all of the things that make up the earth are connected to each other and us, just as we are connected to them. There is truth in the words, "Every action has a reaction." We are just not always aware of what this really means. The consequences are immense. Each time we hurt the earth, we hurt each other and vice versa. When the body is deficient of blood and nutrients, it becomes frail, brittle, and very sickly. The same with the earth. When you remove precious minerals and oil from its core, it becomes frail and brittle and reacts with painful and tragic consequences. Spirituality is not just a human connection. It is an earthly connection, too. Destroying the earth is like destroying one another.

Through these divine messages, I found myself changing spiritually toward life and people. I decided to volunteer myself to anyone who needed help in any aspect of his or her life. This could be spiritual or practical. I would put myself forward to help.

On one such day, a father and daughter asked me to accompany them for moral support to a court appearance for a civil matter. We traveled to Central London by bus early on a very busy morning. There was nowhere to sit; we found ourselves standing very close together. The father asked questions, interested in my spiritual connection. I explained a little about myself, not wanting to reveal too much. I was still not sure how people would react to me, so I kept what I said to a minimum, but even this was enough to keep him enthralled.

The best way I can describe what happened next is to liken it to time standing still. Everything froze around me—except me. A very beautiful voice said, "Blessings, my Son."

When I turned toward the voice, a hand reached over my left shoulder to shake my hand. I took this hand and replied, "Blessings to you, too."

I looked at the source of the voice, a person wearing a long white robe. He took my breath away. He was immaculate, beautiful, not a blemish on his face nor a hair out of place. He was perfection. As he made his way off the bus, I noticed he was carrying something very heavy, almost dragging it. He took small steps because of the load.

My eyes followed him off the bus. People everywhere were getting on and off. I searched for him but could not see him. He had disappeared. How could he disappear in a split second, especially with the load he was carrying? He was hard to miss.

I turned back to my friends. The conversation carried on as though we had never stopped talking. I asked, "Did you see that gentleman who shook my hand?"

"No. What gentleman? We have been talking the whole time."

"He was wearing a white robe, carrying something very heavy and we shook hands and greeted each other."

"We didn't see any such thing take place," one of my new friends said.

Something amazing had happened. I could not stop thinking about the figure and how familiar he seemed. By the end of the day, I was convinced I knew this man. When

I went home, I explained what had happened to Aycan. I could not shake off the feeling that I knew him.

This went on for almost a week, during which I awoke often in the middle of the night, unable to get this out of my mind. Where had I seen him before? There was clearly a message, but I had to work out what it was and why it was consuming me.

A couple of days later, Aycan and I decided to visit my sister. While driving, I talked again about the day on the bus. It had become almost the only thing that I wanted to talk about. Out of the blue, I shouted out, " Oh my God! I know who it is!"

It was Isaac, my guardian throughout my childhood. The same man who meets me each time I have out-of-body experiences, who guides and helps me receive my messages. *He has never left me.*

Both overwhelmed and excited, I stopped the car and turned to my wife. "Aycan, do you hear what I am saying? It was Isaac. He appeared in true form here. He appeared to me. I did not have an out-of-body experience this time, I was totally awake and with other people. I only wish that they had seen him, too."

I was too shaken to continue driving; I needed to allow this to sink in. Just as I was thinking about perhaps the most profound moment in my life, I had another revelation: the heavy load he dragged was, in fact, the heavy burden of the world. That's when I knew he was Isaac, the son of Abraham.

Chapter Five

For the one who has love, peace, compassion,
understanding, strength, and faith:
you will step toward the spiritual light
and in it shall be your salvation.

My **life continued evolving on all levels. I tried to** maintain some semblance of normality in my everyday life, but at the same time, I had to develop spiritually to understand and make sense of what was happening. I found it hard to communicate with many people, because I could not help but imagine that they would think I had lost my mind or was "too out there." It is uncommon for someone you've known your whole life to suddenly say that they have a connection with God. It is natural and human to fear and question what we do not understand; I know that as well as anyone. I would have to be very careful about how, and to whom, I revealed myself. My senses would always tell me if a person was open to this.

I have always considered myself a loving and caring person. I've been known for my sense of humor, sharpened on great British comedy such as *Monty Python, Morecambe and Wise, Tommy Cooper*, and many more. I love to inject a touch of comedy and make people laugh. Thus, it became very difficult for some people to make the connection between Senol, the joker and life of the party, and Senol, the spiritualist.

There were (and are) many people in my life, but only a handful were aware of my gifts and spiritual connection. As time went on, however, more and more people began to witness my out-of-body experiences. I was not yet in control of my gift, so if there was anyone near me who had lost a loved one, and the loved one wanted to relay something to them, it would just happen through me—quickly. This would shock some, even though they were happy. Their loved one would speak through me and pass on messages of comfort and love to them. The person speaking always gave some form of confirmation of their identity. Some who had never seen me in this way would question me about what was happening, both fascinated and supportive. They had known me for years . . . but not like this. Before long, I became known as someone unusual.

Of course, there were and still are skeptics who think that this is all rubbish. What I learned, though, was that the initially skeptical people would contact me when they had lost a loved one. I do not judge anyone for the way they react to me, nor for the criticism I have received. I try not to get into arguments over this because everyone is entitled to their opinion. Before I opened my eyes to my gift, I wanted to be just like them. Sometimes, you have to walk the rocky path before you come to the clearing. This is something that I believe strongly when it comes to spiritual awakening.

On March 13, 2008, at 8:42 p.m., I went out of body again:

> *Blessings, my children. I am Isaac. I speak in a tone of love and without anger. Search your hearts. True love is there, for when you open your heart, you will see before you the one who has love, peace, compassion, strength, understanding, and faith. Look closely into these words, for each word has a meaning. Each will make a new word that will be the key to thy kingdom. Bring yourselves toward the spiritual light and in there shall be your salvation. In this is the key to the gates of heaven.*

A few months later, my wife and I went on vacation with a group of other people. Most I knew well, whilst some were friends of friends. I needed to regenerate myself; a trip abroad would be perfect, I thought.

One day, while relaxing at poolside with a few friends, I noticed a man named Caner, whom I'd only met briefly. He asked if I would like to go for a walk. We waded into the sea. We began talking about things in general, and I told him how happy I was to be with family and friends in Turkey. He then told me that, although I was part of a big group, he could see that I was somehow different from everyone else. He noticed me observing others. He said that, although on the outside I was Senol the fun-loving guy, he thought the way I observed others and took in my surroundings was "different." Unsure how to approach me about this, he had many questions. "What do you want to know?" I asked.

"Everything," Caner replied. "I want to know everything."

I could see that he was genuine. I felt very comfortable talking to him and found myself revealing personal things that only a handful of people knew. He absorbed my words.

While I spoke, he stopped and looked at me with an intense expression. "Senol, you may find this weird, but I have just had a bizarre vision. Just now while we were talking, I have just seen both you and I standing side by side facing a wall."

I understood straight away what Caner meant. I had always felt that one day, I would journey to Jerusalem. I always saw myself and another person standing by my side. This was meant to be. This man was meant to reveal this to me.

Quickly, it was confirmed that Caner was the man joining me to face the wailing wall in my visions. He was not shocked. He said that our conversation had awakened something inside that had been stirring for a long time. It all made sense to him and he believed me completely. It was a very emotional experience for me to know that someone had accepted me totally.

The experience had profound meaning for him, too. He had noticed for some time that a glow surrounded me, and he had been waiting for the right opportunity to speak to me. "I want to help you do what you need to do," he said, "and I will do everything within my means and capability to help you achieve this. You are clearly a very special person and people need to know this. Here we have someone like you in our lives and no one really knows this about you. This is sad."

His words stayed with me, even after our return home. I found myself thinking about what he said. Perhaps the best path of public understanding was to start speaking publicly. I needed somehow to relay the messages coming through to me. Finding the right kind of venue and advertising was important, but left me feeling unsure. I did not realize the amount of work involved, nor the difficulty. I was funding this myself, but I needed to do it, because I believed it would answer so many questions for those interested in spirituality or questioning their own spirituality. Maybe it would open doors for them. Also, it would give skeptics an opportunity to listen to me. Hopefully I would make enough sense to create a connection. Soon, the first day of my first public speaking event arrived. I was very nervous. Had I done all that was needed? Would people even turn up? I was on an emotional roller coaster. I felt I had so much to give, so much to say, but would I be able to convey what's inside? Could I stand in front of an audience and deliver? I was about to find out.

Caner had been true to his word and helped me to organize everything. He told me to remain calm and focus on what I had to say.

Which is exactly what I did. Just before I took the podium, a calmness overtook me. I felt Isaac embracing me, giving me strength. I could see him and other angels smiling. They approved, which meant more to me than anything. This affirmed that I was doing what had been expected and wanted of me for so long.

I had written some notes in preparation, basic words on the topics. I wanted to talk about faith, love, and God. I wanted to share my wonderful divine experiences.

The moment I introduced myself, I realized I'd forgotten to bring my notes. Thankfully, I did not need them. I was given divine inspiration and the words began to flow. I spoke in a calm and clear tone. Anyone watching might have assumed me to be a lifelong public speaker. The audience was deeply engrossed, listening intently, mesmerized. Some were tearful, overtaken with emotion. They told me after the talk that their tears of joy stemmed from the comfort in the knowledge I had conveyed, that their loved ones were very happy and in a beautiful place with other loved ones. I had no problem giving a very accurate description as to awaits us all after we leave this earth. I stayed for some time afterward, happily answering the many questions people asked. Some were so overwhelmed that they invited me to their homes.

It overjoyed me to make such a connection, to deliver words that would change their outlook on life and faith. It amazed me how natural this felt; now I knew why I'd been born. The words flowed like a beautiful, calm river, so natural. I had to build on this.

This is where the hard work began. Caner loved my presentation, but he also knew that there was much more. He knew I could not do this on my own, and he vowed to help and accompany me all the way on the rest of my journey.

Chapter Six

What we hear, is it true?
What we fear, is it true?
So I tell you:
do not fear what is true.

People were talking about me, telling others. I needed
to keep the momentum going. I knew that each time I
talked, I would have to reveal more and more of my experiences. This was the whole point: I had been shown the truth,
and I needed to share it.

Of course, I had some concerns. Some documented
experiences were very powerful and deep, and I did not want
to frighten people. Nor did I want to come across "holier
than thou." That's not me at all. I am human, I make mistakes, and I have weaknesses like everybody else. I would be a
fool not to acknowledge this, but these revelations were still
being given to me to ensure that I revealed them to everyone.
It is very hard to walk that fine line between sharing words
of inspiration and enlightenment. We run the risk of being
labeled a cult or religious leader. Keeping a sense of personal

perspective is vital. My experiences, revelations, and the things revealed to me confirm what my heart already knows: we are all one with God. We are all the same in God's eyes, regardless of faith, religion, color, and cultural background.

I also finally understand that the heart is the key to everything. We are measured and weighed by it—and yes, even judged by it. We should embrace our hearts. They make us who we are. We are capable of infinite love. Within our hearts, most of us want to be better, more loving, caring, and compassionate people, not just to those we love, but to everyone. The small steps we take make the biggest impact on those to whom we give.

While I was organizing my second talk, the Divine spoke to me again. This happened on April 29, 2009, at 10:50 p.m.:

> *What begins and begins again. I take their prayers and I give. Then my children take but do not give. But I still give. As the waters run and as the sun shines I give. Life is just the first steps to true life. Once you leave this plane I smile on what I give. My tears fall like rain and I have not received but I give.*
>
> *You are not perfect, but perfection awaits. When you walk into the light, give yourself without fear. Give without hate. Give love without fear. Give compassion when there is none. Give understanding when there is no understanding.*

I have given you the choice of freedom. My will is your will. Page by page these words are to be read. They are to be absorbed.

I give power and strength in each word. Read and understand these words. To be absorbed. To be read. Enlightenment. I do not punish. I do not give fear. I give salvation. Give and you will be rewarded.

These messages began to grow more profound and meaningful. I was constantly amazed by how much I was learning. Like a child receiving his favorite candy, each experience consumed me more. While these messages were documented, I was guided around heaven. I also witnessed those who had just passed. I witnessed them being welcomed, not just by their angels who had always been with them on earth, but by their loved ones already in heaven. It remains the most powerful and emotional miracle I have ever witnessed.

On one such visit, my guardian Isaac asked me, "Tell me, what you are feeling right now?"

"I am feeling and experiencing real love." Tears of pure joy ran down my face. "Will I be able to give this kind of love to those on earth?"

"It will not be the same as here in heaven, but it will be more powerful than they have ever experienced."

Each time I'm taken away, the experience exceeds the power of the others. I am given the privilege of witnessing heavenly life. On many occasions, I wanted to stay, because while there, I am able to walk around, experiencing everything.

What a realm heaven is! The mountains, hills, and fields are not as you imagine. They are alive; you can feel them. We can communicate with them and feel the energy pulsating from them. I would go as far to say that, telepathically, they speak to you, as one with God. The colors are more intense than any on earth. When you look at the grass beneath your feet, it is an indescribable color of green, so vibrant it almost sings to you and you want to dive in and be enveloped by it. The sounds resonate from a different frequency than anything on earth. The songs of angels are everywhere, seductive in their beauty, so enchanting and mesmerizing you never want it to end. Rivers are unlike any we know here. When you put your hand into the water to feel the flow, the water glistens and shimmers like crystal. Moreover, every time you dip your hand, the sensation is different.

Once, an angel welcomed me, fascinated by the way I was playing with the water. "Is this not familiar to you? It looks as though you have never experienced this before."

I turned and looked at her. "I have been here many times, but the sensation is so beautiful that it feels as though it is the first time."

"The river reacts to you each time. The joy that you feel is multiplied a million times over by the river."

I knelt to the ground, scooped water into my hands, and drank. It is so difficult to describe the sensation I felt. My body began to tingle as the liquid traveled down my throat.

I felt energized. It was of a purity we cannot come close to matching here. I have never tasted anything like it.

Finally, I walked away from the river and came across the most beautiful trees, so proud and strong. I sensed them speaking to me, through their trunks, limbs, and leaves: "Look at how magnificent I am." When they moved their branches, it was like a dance with the breeze, most harmonious.

I continued walking until I noticed that the angel had left. I came to a place of gathering and observed those in place, radiating so much love for all.

During this time, I witnessed the most amazing miracles. One always astounds me: when a loved one passes, those in heaven greet them. It is a very important moment, welcoming a new soul. Those in heaven already know that a new soul will be coming and they rejoice in celebration. It isn't a dying, but a *coming home*. Heaven is already familiar to them, because they have seen and lived there before; this is a "Welcome Home" party!

I realize that a loved one's passing does not feel like a party at all to those left behind. If they only knew what waits for all of us, how our departed loved ones are welcomed, and how happy they are to return home, then it would help with the grieving process. This truth is well worth keeping close to the heart. I have witnessed the passing of many souls. Once they have accepted their own passing, they are happy to return home. They see and feel our tears and grief. They know how much they are missed, and they miss us, too. The difference? They know what we have to look forward to when we pass: joy, peace, love, and happiness. They want us to cry tears of joy, to remember the happy moments, to celebrate their lives, for they know that one day soon, we will all be together. In heaven, there is no time—for them, it will happen in a blink of an eye. For us, it can feel like an eternity.

Everything about a loved one in heaven is illuminated. Beautiful light emanates from them. They appear youthful regardless of their age when they passed. There is not a blemish on them. They are flawless; to see this is a wonderful privilege.

On this occasion, as I continued walking, I came to a tranquil, silent place. Only a few angels were there, but they looked as though they held some kind of authority. I stood by them and began to observe. A scale of some sort stood in front of them, along with what looked like an energy sphere the size of a basketball. It sat on one side of the scale; they were weighing it. At first, I did not understand. The strangest thing was the sound coming from the energy ball. It sounded like a heartbeat.

Suddenly, two very tall, dark figures appeared. They stood and waited. When the scale moved toward them, they took the energy ball and disappeared. I was shocked; it was the first time I had encountered something so bleak. I was tempted to follow them. As I stepped forward, one of the angels put a hand on my shoulder and said, "If you follow, you may not like what you witness. What you will see is the will of God and the balance that has to be kept."

I was not afraid. Instead, a great sadness overcame me. I began to weep because I knew where the two dark figures were going. The angel looked at me. "Do you still want to follow them?"

"Yes." I had to see it and witness it.

She turned and called out to another angel. A very strong male angel appeared and told me that he would go with me so that I could witness, but that I was not to leave his side. "You look familiar," I said.

"That's because I am. I am one of the seven archangels."

We walked together. We entered entering a place that grew more and more distant and dark, nothing like the places that I had visited earlier. A coldness of sorts began to surround me, not what we know on earth, but almost like a nothingness. I began to feel afraid. At that moment, the archangel turned to me and asked if I wanted to continue. I said yes but asked, "What will I see?"

"You know what you will see. You do not need to ask this. Just remain by my side."

We walked until we heard sounds that grew clearer as we closed in on the source. I heard the clanging and grinding of chains and cold iron being slammed against a hard surface. The only light was coming from the archangel beside me.

Terrified and overwhelmed, I grabbed hold of his arm. "We are almost there," he said. It seemed to me as if we were walking forever. He told me to stop. "Are you ready to see?"

Despite shaking and feeling unsure, I replied, "Yes, I am ready."

An enormous iron gate began to open in a 360-degree motion that surrounded us. I could smell . . . death. I never knew a smell could be so foul and obscene, and although I had never smelled death on earth, I recognized it.

As I waited to see what would happen next, two dark figures approached and attempted to touch me. "You cannot touch what is divine, and he is under protection from our Divine Lord," the archangel told them. "He has come to bear witness."

They drew back and remained at a distance, but I could still see them clearly. The energy balls I'd seen earlier now materialized into souls destined for hell. They fell on their knees, sobbing and screaming for forgiveness. From each energy ball more and more souls were falling. I said to the archangel, "Is there no chance that they could be saved?"

"All souls can be saved, but they must truly want to be saved."

I asked him about the chains in the distance. He said that each link represented the pain and suffering inflicted by them on others. When these chains are placed on them, they feel all of it. These chains were no ordinary chains, either. The weight forced them to their knees, and two dark figures dragged each soul along. "What must they do to obtain forgiveness?" I asked the archangel.

"Those in life who have been harmed by these souls will have to forgive them for their terrible sins. Forgiveness is then weighed in favor of the soul who is pleading for salvation, but the request for salvation must come from the heart; that soul cannot lie. If his regret is true and if he is forgiven, he will be taken to a place that is not heaven, but nevertheless is a place of peace, where he can rest and where he will no longer be punished for his sins. It is here that he will remain, but you must know that this place is a far better place than what would otherwise be waiting for him."

All along, I had questioned whether I wanted to continue or ask to be taken back. Nonetheless, it shocked me when the archangel turned and said, "Make your decision." I realized then that he knew every thought going through my mind.

I tried to figure out what I might be required to witness next. I was trembling. "You are safe by my side, but remember, your choice to continue will stir up emotions in you that you do not know exist," the archangel said. "It will make you question how and why the balance is kept, so be very clear in your choice."

I pondered for what seemed like a long time. "Take me forward." I clutched his arm as though my life depended on it while he led me forward.

We were once again surrounded by tortured souls trying to lift their heads and look at us. They were crying from the pain inflicted on them by the chains. The two dark figures beside each would place their hands on the soul's head, forcing it down. One dark figure said to one of the souls, "You cannot look at them. They are not here to save you."

My insides crumbled. I knew why they were here, but it was painful to actually see their suffering. Many times I wanted to shout out "Stop!" but I knew I had to continue walking.

As we carried on, I sensed something behind me. I turned: we were being followed by four very large, dark figures, all formidable and powerful. "Pay no heed to them," the archangel said. "They are attracted to your life force."

I found myself huddling even closer to him. Good thing, because I saw something so horrific it still sometimes comes back to me in nightmarish dreams. Live souls were being torn apart. When it seemed their suffering was over, their beings were put back together—only for the process to repeat over and over again. The dark figures carrying out this torture were clearly enjoying and delighting in their work.

By now, I was crying uncontrollably and feeling very queasy. I looked up and caught sight of someone or something very sinister. He was looking back at me. The only things I could see clearly were his eyes, which sent a terrifying cold chill down my spine. The word "evil" is used on earth quite casually, but in front of me was pure evil. He made sure my eyes were on him; he wanted my attention. He laughed, full of hatred and contempt for all of life and creation.

I could not carry on for a second longer. I turned to the archangel to take me away. Before I could utter the words, he said, "So be it!" and we were gone.

We were back in heaven. The archangel disappeared and another angel came to my side. I was exhausted and still crying from what I witnessed. What I would never forget.

The angel said, "Remember, if they truly repent, then there is a place of peace for them."

These words of comfort arose from an inexplicable truth: God is truly magnificent and always forgives. This experience made me realize the fine balance that God keeps between the earthly and spirit worlds, between good and evil.

Chapter Seven

*Clarity comes when
you have embraced the light.
Light and darkness are one.*

The date of my second event approached. I grew more nervous, because I was unsure as to how far I should go. How much should I reveal when speaking? I was picky about what I wanted to share.

As humans, we are programmed only to take in and digest what we think is of use to us, and we are often limited in what we are capable of accepting as truth. I am very conscious of not coming across as preachy or religious. I wanted my talk to help people feel good about themselves and their lives. I wanted to show them how important each and every one of us is, and how important the role we play here.

I decided it was not the time to reveal my harrowing journey into the backside of heaven with the archangel. However, Caner did not agree. He felt that I should put it all out there. If I was experiencing it, he said, then audiences should know about it. "Those who return time and time again to hear you speak can take what you are revealing," he added.

I was reluctant. I wanted to take small steps. I did not want to come across like a bull in a china shop, and told him so. I wanted to make a connection and encourage people to ask me questions.

I wanted to ignite their curiosity and interest. After many debates, he understood. "We will do it in the way that you feel comfortable. In the way that is right for you," he said.

I had deep respect for Caner. I was pleased that I had someone like him in my corner to discuss these issues but who also understood. He also wanted what was right for me.

The day of the event arrived. Caner decided to record this one. It would be good for me to look back on, he said, for the purpose of improving the way I delivered my speeches. Something so important, after all, had to be delivered in the best possible way. I thought it was a very good idea, because the feedback would assist me greatly. This time, I made no notes. I knew the words would flow easily. As it turned out, I felt at times like I was not the one speaking. I began to talk of the things that came from the deepest part of my soul. Everything I spoke about related to each and every person present at some level or another. I was filled with passion while delivering the words. As I looked to the audience, I noticed a box of tissues being passed from one person to another. At first I was filled with alarm, thinking, *Oh my God, what have I done? They are breaking down in tears!*

but I continued speaking and realized that they connected strongly with what I was saying.

While speaking, I was drawn to the energy of a lady at the end of the third row. She seemed more emotional than the rest, which drew me to her like a magnet. I felt that someone had passed away, someone close to her. Once the talk ended, I walked down into the audience and they surrounded me. They wanted more. It all made sense and they were very comforted. To hear about heaven in the way that I spoke about it gave them so much joy.

Afterward, the lady to whom I'd been energetically drawn approached, still very emotional. She told me she had lost someone very young. "When I heard you speak, it gave me so much comfort," she continued. "It made a very strong connection."

This exchange confirmed I was a step closer to my goal of reaching out to as many people as I could, to bring heaven to their doorsteps, so to speak, to offer true knowledge of heaven and the afterlife. I wanted to awaken them to how truly connected we are to each other and everything around us. I wanted to remove their veils and give them sight. I was succeeding.

On a Sunday night in September 2009, another out-of-body experience happened, documented as follows:

> *I am in heaven, in a field alive with vibrant colors.*
> *It feels wonderful. I want to stay here.*

> *A figure walks toward me. He has an indescribable, amazing aura around him. He approaches and welcomes me. It is Isaac. He wants to share words with all. "I am holding a book. These words are given to you to guide you, to guide all those who are lost. They are words to inspire you, to inspire all. I give words of inspiration.*
>
> *"Everything starts and ends with the heart. Many have lost. Many have been reunited. I will reveal the first step to salvation. To truly know yourself is to make sacrifices in the beginning. I shall show you the circle that takes you to the beginning of life and then to the doors of salvation.*
>
> *"You are like children who read but cannot understand. But to go beyond what you cannot understand, you must recognize when the spirit is free. Follow but do not be led. Lead and do not follow. This is the difference of true believers and those who say they believe. The key: your heart is the beginning. Those who truly believe will understand these words. I leave you now."*

I remembered this experience in detail, even without documentation. That was new. I was receiving immense energy that would surge through my body as if I were being prepared for something. I knew what it was, but as I had been shown, I could not reveal it. I was beginning to grow. I was changing with each experience. My spiritual connection was becoming stronger, and I was becoming more aware of my surroundings. I was more attuned to life.

However, I was also becoming more aware of the shadows, the negative elements around us waiting for the opportunity to pounce when we are at our lowest. I could see their attention was turning more to me, because just as I knew what they were, they knew me and my abilities. I knew that sometime soon, we would clash.

I also knew who was leading them. I call him "the fallen one," but we all know him as the devil. His interest in me was growing. He clearly despised the fact I had a connection to heaven and the Divine, and I was becoming stronger in my faith. He began to test me.

There is good and evil all around us. It is the law of life, like yin and yang, the shadow and the light. There has to be such balance. We have to face the evils thrown at us in all aspects of life, but thankfully, only very few people experience meeting the devil face to face. In my case, I knew he was trying to block me from walking the spiritual path to God. In one out-of-body experience, Isaac told me that I would soon be facing the devil like this. It would be the first of three tests, all of which needed to happen. The first would test my strength, the second my faith, and the third my love for God. Did I have the conviction within me to continue the path chosen for me?

I was about to find out. I could not help but fear what was waiting for me. What would I come across? I was not told when or where this would take place, only that it would happen.

Late one evening without warning, I went out of body. I was transported to a very dark cave, blacker than black. I stood on some sort of rope . . . except it wasn't rope. When I looked down at my feet, the object stretched in front of me, the only thing visible. It seemed to continue endlessly. The crazy thing was that I walked on it without losing my balance. Not knowing what else to do, I continued until I heard a very familiar sound, a very sinister laugh. I knew straight away who it was. There was so much contempt in that laughter but I still could not see him. "So you are the gifted one?" His voice echoed all around me. "Have you recognized my voice?"

"Yes. I know who you are," I replied.

"Then you know what I am capable of, but I will make it easy for you. I offer you the ability to touch and connect with every soul, and they will flock to you. With this will come great power and wealth. I can give you this; after all, this is what you want, isn't it? You want to help those who are in need—the sick, the weak, the poor, children who are lost—who roam this world with nobody to help them. I can give you the ability to save these souls. Just acknowledge me and I will make it happen.

"Look at how you have struggled in your life. You have had nobody to help you, and yet you say God loves you, that He gives you everything. Show me what you think He has given you and I will show you what He has really given you." His voice was full of hatred and scorn, leaving me visibly shaking.

After a moment, I found the words. "If I have to struggle in life and to go without, I know that at the end of it I will have a more beautiful gift than you could ever offer me. I have seen heaven and I have seen the love and compassion that God gives."

Within a split second, he appeared right in front of me, inches from my face, his arms stretched out wide. What I saw next will haunt me for the rest of my life: *all over his body and his arms were screaming, tortured souls, begging for release.* He spat at me. "You turn away from them? Are you prepared to see them suffer? If you refuse me then your family and loved ones will suffer in the same way."

Still trembling with fear, I had to stand firm. "Your fight is with me and not with them. There is a divine order to everything, and even you have to abide by that law."

His face filled with disgust. "Who are you to tell me of the divine law?" His voice elevated into a shout: "I am not bound by this law."

"Isn't denial a sign of weakness? Everything comes under the will of God. It is with His will that I go through this test and face you." I do not know where I found the strength or the courage to speak.

He said nothing. He could only stare, unable to touch me, because he knew that he could not reach me. He wanted my soul so badly. "Return," he finally spat out. "This is only the beginning."

I found myself back in my body, in my home, to find Aycan anxiously asking what had happened, because she had never seen me react like this. She was very frightened for me, unsure what was happening, but aware she could not interrupt or try to bring me back before I was ready.

It took a while to recover. Once I did, I explained everything. I told her how powerful the devil is and what he offered. Tears fell from my eyes; it took her a long while to comfort and console me.

This experience only made my faith stronger. I prayed that God would see it in the same way. I had won this round, but I also feared that the next test would not be so easy. I do not use the word "easy" lightly; it had been the most horrific thing I had ever faced.

I took time to reflect on my life and abilities. I started to wonder what people would think if I told them the full extent of what I experience. How would they react? I tried to see it from the outside, from their angle. How would I react if someone were telling me all this? To be honest, I might ask, "How is this possible? Has this person gone mad?" After all, human nature has shown me that we label and categorize. We tend to judge a person before all the facts are known. I am aware that my experiences were not everyday occurrences. Scholars and scientists would challenge what I have seen and heard at every level, but I knew it to be real and happening to me.

Chapter Eight

The songs I hear are from the heart.
The songs I hear are the start.
The songs I sing will clean
your heart from all sins.

I **received positive feedback from a group of wonderful** friends who belonged to a meditation retreat in Virginia. They had read my writings on a social network and were very interested in what I had to say. Before long, a group member asked if I would be interested in visiting the U.S. to give a talk. "I would love to," I said, if for no other reason but to increase awareness of the messages. The only problem was that I had to fund this myself, as the group was small and unable to help me financially.

But I was looking at the bigger picture. This was a great opportunity to branch out, to make contact with a wide and varied group of people from all over the world. I set a date and left it up to them to organize advertising for the event. With help from my family, I was able to get the money together and book my flight, while my Virginia friends took care of accommodation. I was ready to go.

I arrived in early November 2009 and took a cab to some sort of log cabin resort in the mountainous forest of Virginia. The place looked like a throwback from the past, with no modern amenities. The only telephone sat in the gift shop, and that was for local calls only. The television only played videos, which had to be rented, so for five days I watched the same movies over and over again. I felt very out of touch; I could not even contact my wife in London to tell her where I was and that I was okay.

On the day of the event, my friends contacted me and arranged to pick me up. I was taken to the retreat and thought it was beautiful. It had a very calm and relaxing atmosphere. I felt at home. After introductions, I began to talk. I delivered a wonderful and uplifting spiritual message. They listened intently. I could see and feel that they were connecting with everything I discussed.

It was a success. I felt so happy to connect with people thousands of miles away. They gave me this chance, and it paid off. I am privileged to say that I call many of them my friends today, and for this, I will always be grateful. I am also grateful that I was able to visit one of the most beautiful, breathtaking places I had ever seen.

After five days I returned home, exhilarated. Many more trips to America and elsewhere would follow.

On December 9, 2009, near midnight, I had an out-of-body experience, documented as follows:

I am Isaac. I speak because the time has come for our chosen one to speak. Sounds. Sounds, trumpets, horns, angels sing. Glorious sounds. Songs when he speaks. His words will touch all the souls who will be there. When he stands he shall be removed and we will speak through him, words that will bring joy. Words that will bring love. Words that will bring sadness. These words are truth. There is no turning back. The path is open. Now the time will come for ridicule. Now the time for them to judge and mock but he will stand steadfast. Continue to your last breath. Continue to your last tear. Continue with every drop of blood. Your heart is our heart.

You will need a shield for the rumbling and the stirring of the storm when the ridicule begins. The success of your words makes an impact on everyone's heart. You have not been given this for no reason for you are the reason you have been given and chosen. Love is the hidden true meaning in his word.

Sounds you hear are divine. Horns, divine trumpets, angels. Sounds and songs are what you hear. Speak and they will listen.

This last experience spurred me on; I was very excited. I had been given acknowledgment and an endorsement. I wanted to reach as many people as I could, *now*. I was trying to run before I could walk, and this caused me great frustration. The fact that I financed this alone was a huge burden; long periods of time passed between events. I felt very despondent, because I felt I was betraying God and my gift. There were times when I had to borrow money from my family to put on an event, during financially difficult times for everyone, but I could not be deterred. The words poured through me thick and fast, and my relay to audiences was slow because of the lack of funds.

I found myself questioning my guardians. Why was I given this gift and asked to perform a duty if I did not have the means? Why did I have to struggle? I said, "A little help in some way would go a long way into achieving what is expected of me."

The answer was always the same: that this was a test of my conviction as to how far I would go to make this happen. My struggle was a cleansing process to ensure that there was no ego in my actions. It was not about me, but all of humanity. The rewards, whatever they were, or however they would come, would be beneficial not only to me but to all. I had to ensure that I would put others before myself.

Finally, I understood why I had to struggle. When we are given everything, we do not always appreciate what we have, because we have not struggled nor worked for it. When we struggle to attain our dream, every tiny reward along the way is magnified by our appreciation. It all made sense to me now. This was going to take longer than anticipated, but I knew I would achieve it with hard work and dedication. God and my guardians would be there every step of the way, giving me guidance and comfort. Faith is a powerful weapon.

Six very close friends wholeheartedly believed in me and in what I had to do. Their support was important. They each wanted a role in helping me to secure a reputation with the work I was trying to do. I would meet with them occasionally and discuss ideas and strategies. These were friends whom I had known for a long time and who had all witnessed my experiences, some of which contained something personal to them, such as a passed loved one giving them a message.

I wanted to do a third event, and asked all my friends to come to my house one evening to discuss. I needed them to take more responsibility and become more active. I was very much aware that everyone had their own lives, families, and work obligations, but if they wanted to be a part of this, then they had to provide more input. It was time for action. As we sat around my dining table, ideas began flying around.

As the night continued, I noticed the atmosphere changing. What had started off as a very positive and constructive discussion devolved into a very intense and heated debate. Everyone grew argumentative, disagreeing with each other on all points. This was not natural; this group was tight knit, close. I had never witnessed an argument between them.

I knew straight away what this was: a dark, sinister influence. One negative power instigated this to cause disruption in what we were trying to achieve. I had already been warned that this would happen, and I knew that we all had to remain focused and not be deterred from the path.

The debate became aggressive. Nobody made any sense. I banged both fists on the table, to break the atmosphere, to get their attention. Silence descended. "What is going on?" I asked. "We should not be arguing. Can you not all see what is happening? This is just what he wants: to cause chaos and confusion among us all. He wants to cause a rift between us. We have all embarked on something important. We cannot allow this ever to happen again. We are better than this."

Everyone calmed down. Soon, the negative darkness was gone. We began to focus on our next plan of action. A huge sense of relief came over me that even with what had just happened, we all knew what had to be done.

When they left, I found myself reflecting. This was just the beginning. The closer I got to my goal, the more obstructions would be put in my way. This would not be a bed of roses. Far from it. He would do whatever it took to break me and those I love.

I was responsible for bringing people together to give them a spiritual awakening, to enlighten them and bring them closer to God through the heart, since that connects us all. I wanted to show that God is there for all of us and that we are all one and the same.

When you are doing work that involves bringing people together by talking of love, peace, and compassion, bringing them closer to the light, the dark side begins to take an interest. It wants us all to turn away from the light, to live with pain and suffering, to think only of ourselves, and to turn away from one another. It wants us to turn away from God.

A couple of nights after this, on January 11, 2010, at 8:30 p.m., I went out of body again:

Proof. Look and you will see proof. My proof is everywhere. Look and you will see. Open your eyes and see. The trees, the leaves, the flowers, the clouds, the wind, the rain, the rivers, the seas, the mountains. The water you drink. It gives life. The stars, the planets, the universe, the worlds I have created and beyond that you have not discovered yet.

Proof is there. Do not question. Do not doubt. Do not fear. Open your minds and hearts and see the proof. The power of life given to you from the moment you are able to open your eyes and breathe. There is my proof and yet so many doubt this wondrous thing I have given. Embrace it. Embrace it.

Speak of this and they will listen. Speak with love. Speak with compassion. Speak with open arms. You're the steps. The first of many into enlightenment. Just as the first seed was sown, yours will begin to grow. Begin with these words and it will flow as the rivers and seas sustain the world, your words will flow. This is my truth. Begin with these words.

Each profound experience confirmed what I already knew in my heart. This was not about any one religion, but about bringing everyone together, regardless of race, culture, or religious belief. We are all the same. I am sure that you have heard this before, but at a deeper level, it is about all of us having one heart and one connection. What has been shown to me in my experiences and messages I have received is that there is only one God, regardless of whatever name you call Him. We cause segregation here on earth, but there is no segregation in heaven or hell. Heaven is heaven and hell is hell. I have witnessed this clearly. I have heard and seen God's tears and His sadness at how we inflicted this segregation here on earth, His sadness at how we inflict pain and suffering on one another. I have also witnessed His love and compassion when He welcomes us into His kingdom, and how forgiving He is when we ask. This is not an easy undertaking; far from it. My desire is to bring people together with one voice, one connection. It is what I have been chosen to do.

I am open to anyone, whether Buddhist, Christian, Orthodox, Muslim, Jew, Hindu, or any other religion. I am also here for those who do not believe. It has been shown to me that my love and compassion have to be shared with everyone. When I watch people in our everyday lives, I hear a voice telling me that we are better than this. We are made for so much more. How enriched our lives would be if we all embraced that one connection, so that we were not led or influenced by small-minded people, who narrowly and selfishly seem to want to make a negative impact on our lives.

Now imagine if we embraced that oneness, that connection, that love. This is a huge task. Until now I have never been this open about what it is I have to do because I was never ready. I've been fearful of such an immense task. Now I am ready. Like a boxer prepared to take the blows, I am ready to take the blows that I am sure will come.

Chapter Nine

We begin, we grow
like a seed
laid to ground.
We are watered.
We flourish like a tree.
The tree of life.

I often step back so that I can view the world and see the truth of us all. Through deep meditation, I feel what we have done to each other, what we have done to the world. Once my spirit leaves my body, I travel through many levels. I come to a place of knowing.

On one such occasion, an angel appeared and welcomed me. The light that shone from him was, for want of a better word, amazing. He was Archangel Michael. "Walk with me," he said.

As we walked we came to a very high place of deep divinity and spirituality, full of the most amazing energy. As I watched the world spin on its axis, I was overtaken by emotion, knowing the true power of God and His creation.

I saw the perfection of the world surrounded by equally perfect universes. Even though I know the power of God, every time I have witnessed His beauty, I am filled with reverence and awe.

I turned to the archangel. "We truly do not know what we have been given. Why do we continue to inflict pain and suffering on the world and humanity?"

"So many have turned from the light and closed their hearts. They have allowed ego to rule them," he replied. "Reach out to them. Speak from the heart. They will hear you. No matter what obstacles or barriers are in front of you, if you have faith, the impossible will become possible. There are no limits because it comes from the heart."

I realized then that it only takes one to create the first link of a chain. As each heart opens, the chain becomes bigger. This chain connects us all spiritually, and will keep the world spinning on its beautiful axis. God has not given up on us; He truly does see, hear, and feel everything that we do.

We are capable of so much more. I believe with all my heart that we will be that much more.

Where to begin? It is difficult to break from the circle that keeps us in this life. Our commitments, hardships, struggles, and—above all—fears stop us from looking beyond our comfort zone.

We are not born with fear. It develops later. We *are* born with an instinct to survive—the fight-or-flight response. That is different from fear, which comes from how we perceive things or think of them. When fear becomes a part of us, it often buries itself deeply in our psyche. In some cases, it rules almost everything we do, whether or not we realize it. Some might ask, "How would I be if I had no fear? If I were able to express everything without worrying about the repercussions or reactions from anyone?"

My response: we will always be faced with the hardships of life and our responsibilities. It's how we deal with them that counts.

This is where faith comes in. Faith is the first step of letting go of our fear. It is also the key. Faith is so powerful that it gives us the strength to express ourselves without fearing the consequences. Through faith, we must first cut the cord of fear; then there will be no limits. We can see the world so differently. We can pursue the spiritual path with no ego. Now that would be a true awakening!

Those who are ready and understand fully will follow the light. Those who are not so aware must understand that they need only release their fear.

Fear has been a major obstacle for me for many years because my gift has been a blessing and a burden. For years I doubted myself because I felt I was not strong or brave enough to face this. Each experience is more profound than the one before—and more revealing. As wondrous as these experiences are, they are also very daunting. But I would not change a thing. I would go through every trial and test over and over.

Accepting my gift is one thing, but from a human perspective, I still have my doubts. I don't doubt my gift, for that is perfection, but I ask myself, *Am I strong enough?* I have weaknesses and experience highs and lows like everyone else, but the one thing that has kept me on the path is my faith in God, for God never makes mistakes. I only have to look around and see His miracles in everything. Knowing this gives me the strength to carry on. When I feel His arms around me, I know He is watching over me, which gives me the strength, conviction, and power to move forward. When we move forward, it gives us the strength to meet all challenges head on.

Another experience occurred on June 26, 2010, at 12:25 a.m.:

> *I am Isaac. Dear Brother. Hear these words that I reveal to you. You will walk your path and begin. They will ask, "Who are you?" They will be touched by you. They will cry with you. But they will love you. Chosen are you to carry this. You must accept with your heart. Your name means "life." Your name means "heart." You are heart. Do not turn, Brother. Embrace it. Your tears are the tears of our Divine. These tears of sadness. Do not falter, Brother. Do not doubt. Your time has come. You have asked, "Why?" and yet you have followed. You have followed because of the strength of your faith, of your belief and your passion. You act with love and compassion. Love is the soul. Love is life. Love is the beginning.*

It brings us to face and ask the questions, "Why is there pain? Why is there suffering? Why is there no end?" The answers, as always, will be within yourselves. To love one is beautiful. To love many is divine. To share with one is beautiful. To share with many is divine. To give to one is beautiful. To give to many is divine. But without understanding, without meaning, it is hollow. To be divine is to be full of love for all. Express these in action. Express this by taking the hand of a child. Express this by holding one who needs love.

Share this love. Express by listening to their pain. Express by giving yourself freely.

The bells shall ring and the horns shall rejoice. Speak from the heart. Do not turn away, Brother. Your heart is my heart. Your soul takes the journey. Do not fight it. Embrace it. Speak with passion from your heart. You will be loved. Many shall want your love and compassion. You are all that is good with man. All that is good with God's creation. You are good.

I constantly remind myself about the challenges I will face. How they will come to me? Where will they come from? Who will present them? I am never sure. This is something that I carry with me always. We as humans have the capacity to put the red flag up and run away from something that could be life changing. Our instinct is to doubt or mock anything beyond our understanding or control. If something is not black or white, it can become obscure and vague to us—an uncertainty. If the pieces do not fit, we will discard them. It is easier to discard or forget about something that we do not understand. We replace it with something that sits well with us. For some people, there has to be evidence, something tangible, something they can see or touch, something definite.

For others, even if they have something tangible, they will still question if it is real. Tangible evidence does not always mean that something is real. Even the saying "Seeing is believing" can cause doubt in some. Because of this, the word "faith" has become particularly meaningful for me. Conversely, a blind person does not doubt his senses. He must have faith in everything he experiences. He must have faith in everything he has been taught.

I was given these words of inspiration I would like to share:

> *As he walks through the world, unable to see, he is blind. He can hear and feel, sensing the sounds through his fingers while holding his hands high, wondering what the world could be if he could see. Even without sight, though, he realizes how beautiful this world is that God created and how blessed he is to live here. He feels a breeze on his face. He experiences rain falling on his face, even though he cannot see. He hears the thunder, feels the power of lightning.*
>
> *He then hears a divine voice: "What have you learned even though you cannot see?"*

He answers, "I have learned to be divine. To love from the heart and to know that the only sight I need is not sight, but that my faith and belief is my sight and I see more than anyone can see."

My battle with fear is constantly with me. Every time forces challenge me which want to break my path, I am strengthened by my faith. I am here to do good for all of humanity, and I am well aware that evil forces will play their role. When you are on the path of spiritual enlightenment, evil is always lurking in the corner. Its mission is to upset the balance, to claim as many people for the dark side as possible. I am sure that many others across the world who are gifted or have been chosen face similar battles. These forces do not like love, peace, and compassion. They cringe from anything that is good. They enjoy chaos, panic, and disorder, They thrive on people's pain and sorrow. They want to replace any feelings you have with hollowness, emptiness, and despair. It is never more important to have faith than when you feel at your lowest, when you feel that there is no light at the end of the tunnel. Your strength and your faith will get you through.

Complacency is something that I must never allow on this path of mine, for I must see this beautiful journey through.

Chapter Ten

When we have fallen,
we fall into despair.
When we rise,
we rise with clarity.

A **few years ago, a friend approached me about her** son, about whom she was extremely concerned. It seemed to her that his personality had changed dramatically. He had plunged into a deep depression, though he had previously been an easygoing and free-spirited person. He began drinking heavily and grew short-tempered. Beforehand, this young man lived without any rules, living life to the fullest. He was an extremely musically and artistically talented man who had traveled widely. He loved new experiences, different types of people, and their cultures.

Even though I'd known him since he was a teenager, I had not seen him for a while. I was always left with the impression that he was a very private person, and on the brief occasions that we had encountered each other before this call, I had received no indication something was wrong.

Whenever I asked how he was doing, the answer was always the same: "Everything is cool, sweet."

Which is why I was very surprised, even shocked by what I was hearing from his very worried mother. Apparently, she had asked him for weeks what the problem was, but he was very closed. He did not want to talk about it. Her panic set in when she noticed physical changes in him. He had lost a lot of weight and looked gaunt, as though he had not slept for a long time. Huge blisters began to appear on his body. It was only when she appealed to him that he crumbled and began to explain.

It was quite an experience. He told her about strange and frightening incidents happening to him while at home. Something very dark was awakening him at night, figures surrounding his bed, each more sinister than the last. They threw objects around his room, or he would wake up and not be able to find an item he'd set down the night before. He did not want to accept it at first, which is why it took so long for him to open up to his mum.

Things began to escalate. The figures shook his bed violently, calling his name menacingly and telling him to get off the property. They left no doubt in his mind that they wanted to harm him. The breaking point for him came when a girlfriend stayed the night, only to become so petrified by what she had seen and heard that she fled the next morning, vowing never to return. She did not feel safe until she was far away from the place. By now, he started to have thoughts of suicide.

My friend urged her son to move back home with her and his father until something could be done. He agreed.

She called and asked if she could bring her son to see me. *Of course.* When they turned up, my wife and I were shocked to see his condition. *Was this the same person I had known for years?* He was the shadow of the person I knew.

The moment he walked through my front door, I sensed something very dark and sinister surrounding him. As soon as I looked into his eyes, I knew that he was on the verge of being possessed. I asked him to talk to me. He began to cry, saying that he had had enough and that he wanted to die, that he could not take this anymore. I looked at his mother, her face filled with despair. I took him into my healing room and worked to remove all the negative forces around him, to cleanse him of the evil consuming him. This took some time, but in the end and with God's help, I managed to succeed. I also gave him a spiritual amulet that contained a prayer to protect him at all times.

When we came out of the room, his mother noticed a complete change in him. I explained that it would take some time for him to regain his energy, but he would start recovering straight away and his body would begin to heal. I also made it clear that I did not want him to return to the property until, with their permission, I had dealt with what was going on there. They were happy to grant my request. I was adamant about him staying far away; the prevalent forces were not happy that he had come to me for help. They were not happy that they had "lost" him.

I would soon find out just how angry they were.

After they left, I was spiritually transported into the apartment. What I witnessed was a form of pure evil, full of contempt and hatred toward me for taking my friend's son away. It wanted to destroy the lives of everyone in the family, and was spitting mad at me for taking that chance away. I could not and would not defeat evil, it said; I was wasting my time by going there. "Your comment only verifies to me that you are fearful of me," I replied.

When I came back into my body, I felt very unnerved by how powerful this entity was. It also convinced me that if my friend had not come when she did, her son would have been lost forever. Very soon after, I prepared for my visit to the property and invited two of my spiritual friends to accompany me. The whole apartment was infested by this dark evil force, and I needed their additional spiritual strength to deal with this.

No sooner had we entered the property than we felt the power and anger turned against us. We made our way into his bedroom, the main source of activity. As we began to pray together, the building began to vibrate, making a fearful sound. When we looked down, the floors were moving like ocean waves. Pictures shook from their wall mounts, and the young man's stereo speakers flew off the wall, landing on the other side of the room.

We continued praying to banish this force and asked for God's light, increasing the intensity of our prayer by calling God's name to bless and cleanse this home. It seemed like it took an eon, certainly an hour or more; in truth, it was only about twenty minutes.

Suddenly, we heard an abrupt booming—and then nothing. Complete silence. A feeling of complete calmness swept over us; peace returned to the home. The evil was gone.

We looked at each other, drained and completely devoid of energy. It felt as though we had run a marathon. I could not thank my friends enough for being there, and they thanked me. Then we all thanked God for his blessing and protection and for aiding us in saving this soul. Before we left, we tidied up and hung some prayers on his wall.

Not long after, my friend's son contacted me. He sounded full of life, with a vibrancy I had not heard in a while. He told me he would be moving back into his home, but not before taking some time to travel in South America. Seeing him back to his former self and ready to take on the world was reward enough for me; it put a big smile on my face.

Even though I had dealt with this kind of phenomena in the past, this particular experience was one of the worst, more so because the victim was somebody I knew. This was not a spirit that needed to be moved into the light, but a darker, more powerful force, an entity with a very strong energy source.

These types of entities need hosts to thrive. It will latch on when the unsuspecting host is at their most vulnerable or weakest. It feeds off of that energy and emotions while carrying on a life of its own, a discarnate energy pattern with malicious intent. It can be unpredictable and controlling, and use violence toward its victim. When it chooses its host, it takes away their peace of mind. The victim might feel as though they are losing themselves, which in a way they are. Depression, anxiety, addictions, and even suicidal tendencies can result. Insomnia ensues because you are afraid to sleep. The personality can change completely. Sometimes, physical changes occur, as they did with my friend's son.

The more energy the entity draws from a person, the stronger it becomes. Energy is an entity's superfood. It not only controls the person, but his or her surroundings. Hence the throwing of objects around the room.

Those who experience these things must not be afraid to speak, to tell someone close. The moment you share, you show the entity that you have the strength to fight off consumption by it. I would also like to point out that you may not be aware that the cause is an entity, but may be aware of chronic changes to yourself and your home. The good news is that an entity can be released and removed effectively, but you also have to find the strength to stand up to it. Let it know that you are in charge of your life.

Chapter Eleven

Death of a light
is death of an angel.
Rebirth of a light
is rebirth of an angel.

Another out-of-body experience occurred on July 7, 2010, at 10: 26 p.m., again involving Isaac:

You will feel the pain of many. But you will shine as the sun shines. I shall give you love and you shall share this love. I shall give you words to share with the many. Water is the giver of life, as it flows through mountains, rivers, and seas. Rain falls through the skies giving life, giving sustenance.

The heart sends blood through your veins, giving you life, giving sustenance. Your lives are connected to each other here on earth and to the Divine. Only when you become the divine spirit and you walk through the Divine's gardens will you know this. You will see the divine light that links us all to the one heart. Many say they have seen this. Many say they have touched this, but do they understand? Only one with a true heart will. There are those who seek love. There are those who seek connection. There are those who follow without question. There are those who follow to ridicule. There are those who say they are your friends. You must all decide if their hearts are open.

You must always walk into the dark with love in your heart, then you will see the light, the Divine.

It frustrates me to see and feel the events of the world unfolding. It breaks my heart that most of humanity has become so detached and uncaring. God has made it clear to me that a time of change is in our hands. He witnesses the atrocities inflicted on a daily basis to innocent children, men, and women around the world. God did not create segregation. We did. For every child that is killed, we murder innocence and a potential good in the world. Each time a child is killed, an angel dies. Not only was this revealed to me, but I have witnessed it. It is the saddest thing for anyone to see. An angel walks with a child until adulthood; at that point, it moves to a newborn child. If a child is killed before it reaches adulthood, then that angel dies, too.

We are responsible for everything we do. The consequences of every good or bad deed is felt in heaven. I have seen the sadness of the angels when terrible events occur on earth, whether natural catastrophes or manmade tragedies that take many lives. Angels feel those vibrations. Their light begins to dim. They stop and put their hands across their chest. The sadness they feel is very deep. They bow their heads in a somber way and pray until their light grows stronger and they begin to prepare for the incoming souls. I see the love in them. They are rejoicing, too, for family is coming home. They will console and help with the soul departing earth.

Even though we are grieving, they are rejoicing for the new arrivals, while praying that the catastrophes and tragedies will stop.

Many people question why God does not act and put a stop to all of this. Why does He allow these catastrophes to occur? Why does He not show Himself and say, "Enough is enough"?

God has given us the greatest gift of all—free will. Killing and inflicting pain and suffering is not allowed by God. But we have allowed it. We have the capacity and the will to stop. We have the power and will to change things and to put it right. This is our responsibility on earth. The easy thing is to pass it to someone else and let them deal with it. The right thing is to make a change happen for yourself.

When you can change yourself, you become able to help others change, too. Change is the key for all of us. I have witnessed the profound transition to our lives in heaven, where we become a light full of love and compassion. It does not matter who we were or our ethnic or cultural backgrounds. It does not matter what religion we practiced or what language we spoke. In heaven, everyone is referred to as brother and sister; there is no prejudice. There are no differences what-soever. We are all the same, with a strong unbreakable link to each and every soul. I am always deeply moved when I witness this.

While writing this, however, deep sadness grips me, because we do not have that unity currently among us. We can do something about it. We do not have to wait for heaven. We do not have to wait to pass before we feel that connection. We can create it here. It is what is expected of us. The phrase "heaven on earth" is used for a reason. We choose to be blind to it, but I am no longer blind because of what I am seeing continuously.

The change I have made is revealing to you the heav-enly messages given to me. These messages are not meant to frighten or judge, but to enlighten everyone. They are intended to open your hearts to a wonderful world that has always been there: our eternal home. You will be totally free, with no restrictions or fear. Children can run and play, their laughter infectious, and no one worries about time. Time does not exist.

When I am in heaven walking among everyone, the sense of freedom awes me. It cannot be compared with what we think of as freedom. I have never climbed a mountain in my life, but if I see a mountain in heaven and want to climb it, I have the ability to do so. The sensation of knowing that you can do anything, even strenuous and difficult activities, is exhilarating.

I have been given the privilege of experiencing how passed souls live in heaven. It does not matter how poor or how rich you were. Everyone is equal. There is no status. You can have the home of your choice. That's right—there are homes in heaven. Whatever is in your heart becomes your home. If you dream of a home surrounded by a river or trees, hills or mountains, then you will receive it.

In heaven, a beautiful harmony surrounds everything and everyone. Everything just flows. Everything reacts to the love of each soul. If a soul is elated, then his or her surroundings become magnified with that elation. A human eye cannot see these vibrations, but you'll see them in heaven, flowing with the connection each soul has with another. It is a wondrous sight, one I have never gotten used to.

Every time I visit heaven, I experience a new and wonderful revelation. Many times, I have walked in the fields, totally at peace. Knowing nothing and nobody can harm me. When I shout at the top of my voice with joy, angels stop, look, and smile. They know the happiness I feel. Many times, angels have sat with me in the fields and spoken. I always ask them about heaven and earth. My questions are endless. Once I asked, "Why is life on earth so hard?"

An angel replied, "The hardship was created by humans. It never had to be this way. The first hardship was when man began to segregate. Man made the choice to do this."

"Humans have always looked to God to help us in our time of need and struggle. Why does he not intervene?"

"God has intervened numerous times in the past and yet it became apparent that you do not learn from your follies," she said. "You become dependent on God to put right all the wrongs that humanity has done. God has given you all free will and has made a pact that He will not interfere in anything that you do. He has left it in your hands to do the right thing. God sends angels to whisper in your ear. You call this your conscience. These angels are there to give you warning or advice when you are about to make a wrong turn in your life. You just have to listen to it."

She followed with a simple example about what people like to call "coincidence": "You could walk down the same road at the same time every day, and one day for no reason at all you might decide to take a different route," she explained. "You find out later that some kind of accident or catastrophe has occurred on your usual route. You stop and think and say to yourself, 'Something told me to take a different route today. I do not know what or why, but I did.' This you call your conscience, but it is an angel whispering to you and telling you to take a different route. This is something that happens continuously. God sends out angels to do His work in this way. He is not interfering, but subtly speaking to your soul."

Her revelations mesmerized me. What fascinates me even more is that she and other angels are equally mesmerized by me. I have told them, "I do not understand why you look at me in wonderment."

One angel replied, "It is not only because of the divine gift that God has given you and that you sit here among us, it is also because of your life force that shines so brightly. We are drawn to it because it reminds us of what it was like when we lived on earth."

"Do you mean that you were once human, like me on earth?" I asked.

"Yes. There are some angels who once roamed the earth in human form. Their task was to spread the word of love, peace, and tolerance to all."

The one thing that constantly stands out is the love emanating from these angels, no matter what mistakes and wrongs we do here on earth. They always love us. They look upon us as their children. Children can be mischievous or misbehave, but this is not the case for terrible sins. For these, the punishment will be just.

Listening to and learning from angels has shown me that all is not lost. There is hope. The one thing that links us all here on earth is our humanity. All we have to do is believe and have faith. The angels have not lost their faith in us. They hold hope, and they never stop praying for us. I see the love in their eyes when they speak of hope for us. They have not given up on us. Neither should we.

Chapter Twelve

I give you hope and faith
and they walk hand in hand
and they will never break.

Isaac returned when I went out of body on July 27, 2010:

I have come to give you these words to inspire you and share with others. Remember to love, give, and not to expect. Just give. Open your arms, embrace all that comes. Love all. You shall not fall. You shall overcome. You shall walk high. Your voice will be clear. Each step you take will become a stride. Many will want to hear your voice. Your heart, your love, your compassion. Give this to all. Speak with emotion. Speak not from paper but from the heart. Angels are everywhere. Guardians follow. Each soul has its own guardian. Only those who are chosen can see them. You will love many and you will help many. Just give your hand to them and listen.

This small act of compassion is divine. Give without hesitation, without thought. Give your heart. Give with

*all you have. To love one is beautiful. To love many is
divine.*

It takes me some time to actually come back into my
body. From the perceptions and comments of witnesses, I
seem to be in a deep trance, like sleep. This is when I am
being guided around heaven. Many times in the past, I did
not reveal what I saw when I returned, because I wanted to
keep my experiences to myself. Now, through writing this
book, I can share those revelations.

After one of my experiences, I revealed what I witnessed.
A friend wrote it down verbatim:

> *Two angels welcome me. Isaac stands with them,
> really happy to see me. I am happy to see him. He is such
> a pious person. I fall on my knees every time I see him.
> He says he's going to help me complete what I have to do
> when I find it difficult to speak. Then the angels say they
> would like to take me somewhere, and to follow them.
> Isaac smiles, filling me with emotion. You can see God
> through his smile, through his face. He is filled with so
> much love. "Go with the angels," he says, "and reveal
> what you see."*
>
> *Beautiful fields surround me. As I crest a hilly ridge,
> an amazing city appears suddenly. It goes on and on,
> angels everywhere. I move closer and see families of
> those who have passed. Whole families share food with
> each other, laughing, enjoying heavenly life and assorted
> activities—sitting, eating, watching children play.*

Angels play among them. All I can hear are beautiful heavenly songs that melt my heart and make me want to cry, but not tears of sadness. As I walk among them, they smile, welcoming me. It feels like I have never left. "It has always been there. It has always been there," I say to the angels.

"Faith is all you need, and you will witness heaven," one replies. "You will know it has always been there." As I fight back tears, another says, "We are going to take you to meet someone."

I walk into a vast open space. The divine energy is very strong. Even the grass, trees, and breeze feel different. Then the Archangel Gabriel appears. "Follow me."

I walk with this huge figure, his wings expanding far and wide, his hand on my left shoulder. He shows me the other archangels: Michael. Raphael. Azrael. I see them all, these saints. Each wears a sort of armored uniform. They look magnificent. Other archangels surround them, all towering figures, so powerful. Their wings expand so broadly that it seems I'm looking at thousands of them. An awesome sight.

The archangels acknowledge me by bowing their heads. I do the same. "Do you feel fear standing among us all?" Gabriel asks.

"No. I am just in awe of their magnificence."

I feel the divine power they possess to fulfill their roles, their missions. Gabriel extends his hands, inviting me to walk among them. In a very calm and authoritative voice, Raphael then asks Gabriel, "Does he understand the gift that he has been given and how blessed he is to be walking among us all? To see us in our divine robes?"

"It is not for us to question our Divine Lord's invitation to the one who is gifted," Gabriel replies.

Soon, I found myself back in the field where it all started.

Many times, I have been asked to elaborate on the purpose of these experiences and revelations. "Do I understand what is happening to me?" people want to know. It has taken me many years to finally understand that the purpose of all of this is a calling, not just as a human being, but on a spiritual level. A calling to pass on these revelations to all who seek spiritual awakening, bearing the knowledge we are not just running around without purpose.

It has been hardest for me to face the fact that I had to reveal this to everyone. I travel to heaven and back and then have to tread very carefully in how I reveal this. To tell people how they should walk through life can come across as condescending and judgmental, truly not my intention. What I am trying to do is share the true meaning of life.

What occurs here on earth is connected to heaven and witnessed. God responds accordingly to each and every act, good and bad. I have grown to understand that through these revelations, our pain, suffering, and despair do not go unnoticed.

We must have the ability to acknowledge the existence of God within us. He is there. He is everywhere. Open your hearts so that you can hear Him, feel Him, and see Him. Know that His divine grace will guide us. I dream that one by one, all of us will experience the divine light here on earth.

I might view this world differently because of my experiences, but it is very important to understand that I am the same as everyone else. I have my fears and doubts. My biggest fear is how people will view me. I know that I will face many questions. I know that I will try to be disproved. What I have experienced and am sharing does not conform to what many people see as normal.

All who have written about their spiritual journeys have probably felt the same as I do.

Science will always try to find an answer. When they cannot solve the question, they leave it open and call it "unexplained." I find this a miracle in itself. For every one question or scientific experiment that has no answer or solution, God plays a part.

We have all watched programs about the history of man and how we came to be here. We now know of our ancient ancestors and the rituals they performed, and who they worshiped and perceived as Gods. With today's technology, scientists are now saying that these ancient people were probably aliens. If they were aliens, then *who created them?*

I know God has created everyone and everything. God is the last being whose existence scientists will admit. They dedicate their lives in the pursuit of truth, but often steer further away from it. The truth is and always has been there in front of them.

Chapter Thirteen

From out of darkness
you will see the light.

I wake up each morning knowing that I am closer to my goal. I can feel my guardian's sense of happiness that I have begun my journey, revealing the beautiful message that I receive. This gives me serenity and euphoria, together. I feel as if I want to open my front door and invite everybody in. I have accepted that I need to grow and my struggles are a very important part of this, for it is in this understanding that I will step forward to my own personal glory.

Likewise, understanding ourselves is one of the first steps to awakening. Accepting the need to grow within yourself will bring you closer to the divine. Taking that step forward to opening your hearts will bring greater heavenly glory. As for religion, I have been asked many times, "What is its purpose?" Is religion not supposed to make you into a better person? From my perspective, the purpose of religion is to create a connection to God, to enable you to remember Him in your day to day life, to acknowledge His existence in every action you take, to carry Him in your heart the way He carries you in His arms. It is the means by which you become the best person you can be, knowing that He forgives us, and then learning from those mistakes. The message of any religion is to give love, peace, and tolerance to every person who needs it.

The beautiful unity and harmony I have witnessed in heaven many, many times is what we could experience and celebrate here on earth. For me, witnessing this is the single most powerful experience I have ever had, and what I wish for the most.

We are capable of so much greatness, and blessed with the ability to make it happen. The first step is to start within ourselves, allow ourselves to grow, and accept the light into our hearts. Know that God is great and that He looks out for each of us. Our well-being is what matters to Him, giving ourselves to the light. When we have done this, we will view the world and all its beauty in a wondrous way.

On September 15, 2010, at 1 a.m., I had an out-of-body experience, documented as follows:

> *Feeling the vibrations, healing vibrations. Feeling the vibrations, sensing, pondering path in front. The path is laid. You have light to guide you. You have our hands to guide you. You take so much. Express this with love. Remember, you must break the twigs to allow the roots to grow. As the leaves and seed pods fall to the ground, they become seeds, and these seeds begin to grow,*

reborn, fragile. They grow to be tall, strong, and beautiful beyond imagination. To see only as the few who have the ability to see. Look and see how you have grown. You are of age. Grow like a tree. Spread your arms and words as a tree spreads its branches.

I have been with you from the beginning. I took your hand and acknowledged you and you acknowledged me. Remember to speak from the heart. For to speak without the heart has no meaning. Use words from the heart. To speak from the heart is linked to the divine light. You have been given the divine gift of having the belief in each soul.

All of my experiences are enlightening on many levels. Each is different, each a miracle. Some I have kept even from my wife—until now.

One day, I was alone in my spiritual room, preparing to meditate. A deeply divine, commanding voice called my name. Although it was familiar, I couldn't quite place it at first. I turned toward the voice; in front of me stood Archangel Michael. He wanted me to go with him. "Do not question. Follow me, my son."

I followed. While my physical form was still in the room, my spiritual body walked with Michael toward an amazingly beautiful light, which I recognized. We stood together in a portion of heaven I had not seen before, surrounded by mountains so magnificent they drew me in like a magnet. I could not take my eyes from them. They vibrated with the sound of a thousand people chanting in unison.

We continued walking until I turned to him and stared. Michael looked glorious. His beautiful robes hung in such a way to outline his magnificent physique. He stood so tall, proud, and perfect, and the light that shone from him was pure and mesmerizing. His eyes filled with love and compassion; they were humble, with no trace of ego. "I understand why you are the protector and healer," I said.

He looked at me and smiled. "Come. There is so much for us to talk about."

We arrived at what I can only describe as a cove, a cut-out almost, a horseshoe shape. I could hear water but I couldn't see it. The place was very calm and tranquil. He invited me to sit beside him on a grassy verge.

Michael put his arm on his knee, rested his hand on his cheek, and looked at me. He began observing me quietly as if waiting for me to speak. But I didn't. A few moments of silence passed before he said, "Have you learned the names of the angels that walk in human form?"

I knew what he was asking. There were people who came into my life for this reason. When I looked into their eyes, I would know them in a spiritual way. Their belief and support of me was without question. "Only two, but I do not know all of them as yet," I said. "I know that I will meet them in time."

"They will be revealed to you in due course."

"Why have you asked me this?"

"You need to know the names of the angels who are going to support you," Michael replied.

"I know of one angel, Isyll, who has supported me without question, and whom I have a very strong bond with. The other is a male, Amed. I also have a very strong bond with him, but he is in conflict. Not with his support of me, for that is unquestionable. His conflict is with himself and others around him."

"When you begin to reveal to him, he will know his name and he will come to you, with no conflict."

I turned to Michael. "There is so much I would like to ask you but I do not know where to begin."

"Speak. Ask whatever comes from the heart."

I was ready to ask, *When God created hell, what did you and the other archangels truly feel?*

Before I could, Michael answered, "He created truth. Everything He does comes from the truth. Everything our Divine Father has created is with truth, to restore balance. When the fallen one questioned our Divine Lord, He created hell. The fallen one questioned everything our Divine Father did and asked Him why He gave so much love and blessings to His creation. He questioned why our Divine Father gave humans so much esteem, so our Divine Father gave free will to restore balance. I as well as others challenged the fallen one. Why does he question our Divine Father? But our Divine Lord spoke and allowed the fallen one a choice, to make a covenant between Our Father and the fallen one.

"It was agreed that whoever chooses to follow our Divine Father may follow Him, but that whoever chooses to follow the fallen must follow him. This must be decided by mankind's own free will. This was agreed; this was written. I asked our Father to destroy him and not give him this covenant, but his answer was to give free will. The fallen one was angry with this action and he was banished from our kingdom."

I looked at him, amazed. I wanted to know so much more. Once again, the archangel Michael read my mind. "We will talk again. You must now return to your earthly body. Take these words with you and remember them. It will give you strength and conviction in the work that you will do. These words are not for the select, but for all."

We walked back toward the light. Before I entered it, I turned, reluctant to let him go. "I love you and all of the angels. I am truly blessed to have been given these beautiful miracles." He smiled.

I started walking through the light and slowly found myself back in my body, in my spiritual room, in the same position as if I just walked in there to prepare for my meditation.

Chapter Fourteen

True change comes from within.
True strength comes from the heart.
Together we can overcome our fears.

I **often hear people questioning heaven, or seeking irre-**
futable proof of it. First of all, and contrary to popular
belief, there's no physical blueprint of heaven that you can
print on a page, like a colossal map. Heaven lies in our hearts
and souls. It stretches forever around us. It is the small voice
or sound deep inside which every now and again nudges us
with a guiding hand, reawakening us.

Our souls know that heaven exists, because that is where
we come from. The heart is a life giving force to our bodies
but also the key to the Divine Kingdom. So simple, yet we
take it for granted. The functioning heart, pumping the
blood through our bodies, is the invisible force that connects
us to our aura.

When the body dies, that same force continues. It takes
us to the kingdom of heaven and regenerates us. It's like a

skeleton key that opens all doors. It is with us from before we are born and stays with us for eternity.

Heaven is tangible. I have seen it, smelled it, heard it, tasted it, and touched it. I have walked among those who have passed and I have walked among angels. Each time I have been privileged to visit, the experience is even greater than the time before.

Faith is our most important stepping-stone to heaven. The unity and wonder of this place proves our faith. Everything works with perfection, everyone knows who they are, and there are no commands or directions. We just know. Peace and tranquility flow beautifully, leaving us feeling cleansed. We realize we are one complete body made from trillions of souls.

On January 10, 2011 at 10 p.m., I went out of body again:

> *To stand alone. To observe the world. To see how life continues. To see a child being born. To hear its first cry. To hear the comfort of its beating heart. This is the child's connection to the Divine. This sound is the beginning. This sound is the end when we leave this body. this sound we hear when we begin a new life. We search, constantly wondering, "Is it true? Is it real? Few of you believe and many of you doubt. Only when you hear the sound of God in your heart when you sleep do you understand the connection. Every beat is a song, the sound of great drums that beats in all of you. So put your hand*

on your heart and feel that connection. Listen to its beat.
Then say, "Yes I feel the beat. I feel the true beat."

The core of these wonderful miracles and messages is that we are truly one body. We are shown this in full clarity when we pass. When in heaven, I have witnessed a soul's reaction to this clarity. It is not unfamiliar, because our souls have always known it. They are glad to be home, because their lives in heaven are a continuation of what they knew before their earthly life.

It is as if they never left. To see that joy, that light which shines from them, is the most wondrous feeling in the world. As I walk among these souls, I see continuous love and joy spreading as they work together in unison, constantly welcoming newcomers, embracing and enveloping them with tenderness. They share stories of their memories and lives on the earthly plane, smiling and laughing when something amusing is shared. They shed tears over sad memories. The sadness is never because they are sad, but because of the way these life experiences are shared in heaven. For newcomers, it is like a form of therapy; for those who welcome them, it is a show of empathy. This enhances the love that they have for each other. It is not just the welcoming of family and friends that enhances this love, but also the realization that they become part of one big family. Humankind, uplifted into heaven.

When I am there and witness this, I become part of it. At moments like these, I do not want to return to this earthly plane. Not that I want to leave earth or my loved ones, but only on earth do we feel the pain and hardships of daily life. That pain does not exist in heaven.

Sometimes, I walk alone through the beautiful gardens, watching children play. Angels appear by my side, easy to identify by their appearance and light that emanates from them. Sometimes they ask me for my thoughts. On one such occasion, I answered, "Can there ever be this kind of love and peace on earth? Can there ever be this kind of unity that is so clear here?"

"All mankind has the ability to enjoy peace and love on earth because it has always been there within you all," one replied. "This can happen when you realize that there are no differences between you. You will never be able to create heaven on earth, but you can create something truly wonderful."

Her words left me with great hope, though I knew that this would be a task more easily said than done. This made me even more determined to share my experiences and to do something, whatever was in my power, to make the world a better place.

As human beings, we are led by fear. Fear plays a big part in our daily lives, the fear of what we do not under-stand. Apprehension and the fear of change hold us back from what we really want.

Changing our whole way of thinking and life is a huge step. What we do not understand is that, once we want to change ourselves, not only can we change, but we see the benefits and begin to care for and help others. We no longer hesitate to make a difference. Suddenly, we *want* to help the world. A positive cycle begins. By putting our hands out to one person, letting them know they are not alone, and allowing our humanity to shine through, we reveal great willpower and inner strength.

Chapter Fifteen

To walk in heaven
and feel the love beneath your feet.
To walk on earth
and feel the sorrow beneath your feet.
To walk as one
and feel His embrace.

I wake up every morning more energized and excited by the prospect of sharing my thoughts and feelings with others and bringing them together. Today this feeling is stronger than ever. I have been through so much, and I have experienced and witnessed so much. This energy grows consistently in me; it has made me strong, determined. The excitement I feel comes from being of help in any way possible. It is just the beginning for me, not just here on earth, but on a spiritual level also.

I have only experienced a small piece of heaven; I have yet to experience and see much more. The best part of my journey is yet to come. Ever since I accepted and embraced this path God set out for me, I have felt a reward which has nothing to do with money or material things. When I help, the happiness or relief on a person's face serves as my reward. I feel their love, and that is priceless, but the greatest rewards are the gifts I receive from God. That He has blessed me with continuous glimpses of heaven and the afterlife is truly a blessing. What I have learned from these journeys has enabled my soul to grow and understand how wonderful life on earth would be if only we all knew and understood.

I am no different from any other man or woman. I have made mistakes, but all mistakes, great or small, are lessons within themselves. There were times when I relied too much on others to help me in my endeavor. I expected them to be there for me as I had so often been there for them. I expected them to understand my passion for the work and to help me make it happen. If it was not working, I would blame them rather than myself, not taking into consideration that everyone has priorities of their own. I was too consumed by what was happening to me and I was desperate to "put it out there."

A huge turning point for me was in understanding the difference between a person offering help and being support-ive, and my own expectation that they would do everything for me. Changes can only come from ourselves.

After a lot of soul-searching, I hope and believe that is what I have done. I have grown as a man both spiritually and intellectually, and my senses are so in tune with everybody I meet that sometimes it is almost too much to contain. When I am in a crowd of people, I can feel their sorrow, anguish, anger, and pain. I feel as if I am carrying all of their burdens on my shoulders. I can feel the despair inside of them, many having lost faith due to the daily struggles of life. In those instances, I have a strong desire to embrace them, to open my arms and tell them that I care, to not give up on themselves or each other, because it can change. We can change.

Millions of people across the world live in oppression. We are often robbed of dignity and hope when our daily lives are dominated by material, economic, and political struggle. Logic and reason become non-existent, because we are constantly being told that our lifelong neighbors are now our worst enemies, the very people we must now fear.

I strongly believe that the leaders of the countries where atrocities and injustices occur are afraid. They fear their people waking up, or indeed, having a spiritual awakening. Can you imagine one person holding out their hand to a neighbor or family member with a different belief and saying, "Take my hand, Brother. We are one."

Regardless of where we begin, we are not different from one another. In heaven, not one person oppresses nor steps on another. There is no division, no divergence of belief.

In my experiences, it has been revealed to me that humanity is heading to a very dark place. I was in the garden of heaven with Archangel Michael when I was shown a scenario where the whole world will be engulfed in death and destruction if we do not change our ways. I shook with fear and desperation, because I thought that we as humans might not have the strength to turn away from this terrible end. I looked at Michael with a feeling of despair and sadness, my mind screaming for answers as to how we can change. He knew what I was asking, and so he continued to reveal to me that I was not the only one in the world to receive this gift.

Others are walking the same path as I am, waking up to the duty ordained for them. Michael told me that when the time comes, I will know them and they will know me. Together, we will help humanity to embrace peace and light.

Through these revelations and spiritual encounters, I have learned to become aware of the humility needed on earth. We all have it. We must not allow things to escalate out of control and refuse to act. We must not bury our heads in the sand.

I have thrown myself completely into reaching and connecting with everyone, to help bring everyone together. Each time I think of my task I am very moved because I am hugely aware of the responsibility that I have.

As I embark on this incredible journey, I wonder what people will think of the revelations in this book. I have no idea what will be expected of me when I encounter many different people. What will people ask of me? Will I be able to handle this huge weight and burden that I carry? The most important thing for me is that people recognize and embrace the things that I can teach them.

God did not create us to harm each other. God created us with the ability to know our own wrongdoing. He looks upon us with love and sorrow. He will not intervene, even if we allow ourselves to go to a point of no return, because He has so much trust in us that we will turn around to choose the right path and do the right thing. He also made us equal. We are the ones who have created injustice and inequality. We are God's children. So far, He has not given up on us. Why wait until we leave this physical body to see the wonderment of heaven when we can feel and experience it first, here on earth?

One night after a spiritual talk, I was mingling among the guests, amazed by their reactions. I spoke with each, and each acknowledged and understood what they had received. It still warms my heart, because I remember their emotional response. They told me how much they connected with my words, how they made so much sense. They understood that everything we do is connected to the Divine and that we are accountable for our actions. It gave me a feeling of hope for the future and a sense of personal and spiritual achievement. It verified that I can connect with a handful of people and make a difference. One drop can become a river. A river can become an ocean.

We are all blessed with spiritual light, but so many have walked away from it, knowingly or unknowingly. When we have doubt, we expect God to put us right, to show us the way. God has never turned His back on us. He is always there in our highest and lowest moments. He wants us to use what He has given to make changes, to make a difference, and to make something of our lives, regardless of our background or situation. Good things will always happen when we acknowledge and accept this.

On March 8, 2011, at 10:15 p.m., I went out of body:

There is a beginning to all forms of life. There is a growth in all forms of life. There is learning, there is joy. There is suffering, grief, and pain in all forms of life. Man has been made to endure this. Only man can endure trials and burdens. We have been created this way. We constantly ask, "Why?" All those connected to a spiritual understanding will know. All those who know will accept these trials and tests and will know what our Divine Father wants from us.

To be able to walk on this earth and understand the meaning of the earth beneath your feet. To touch with your hands the soil, to smell it. To hear vibrations from the mountains, to hear the earth living and breathing reacting to everything—as we bleed or when we are wounded so does the earth bleed.

When the earth shakes it leaves the wounds we inflict upon it and yet man continues to not hear these sounds and not see the signs. Only those who feel from the heart know this to be true, those who know that the spiritual light carries love and compassion. You may ask how you can all change. The answer is there in your hearts. It is easy. Take the first step and this is how it begins.

Chapter Sixteen

The end is never the end.
It is only the beginning.
The journey continues . . .

This is how it started. First man and first woman, Adam and Eve, were in the Garden of Eden. God said they could enjoy all of paradise, for He had provided them with everything that one desires. The only stipulation to this blissful state? They could not pick the fruit of a specific apple tree—Tree of Knowledge. This was the first true test of faith. Both Adam and Eve failed, because they used their free will to pick from the tree. They were cast from paradise into the world, which began what we know as the struggles of life. They had to fend for themselves in a very harsh environment.

As time went on, human beings developed and populated the world. Man began to see himself as something bigger. In that moment, the ego took over and chaos ensued. Throughout the history of man, we have continued to wreck, destroy, and destruct. We never think or feel that every action has a reaction. I constantly ask myself, "How long can we continue on this path?"

Every time something is killed, we die a little. Although it seems as though so many have lost the ability to hold or live through faith or a spiritual connection, I believe this not to be true. It is in all of us. It is just that so many have forgotten.

I know there is a big, beautiful light at the end of the forgotten tunnel, because, slowly but very surely, more and more of us are asking questions and becoming spiritually aware. When this happens, your faith begins to develop. Some may call this hope. I call this a divine awakening. Soon, it will happen in a very big way, because what binds us all, what truly brings us together, is something we all seek: love.

I finally find myself at my true starting point, the divine path. Now all I have to do is walk.

In one of my documented experiences, I described a divine pen. I had never seen anything like it. The top of the pen extended upward into infinity. Endless words appeared from its tip in a fluid motion, words from *The Book of Life*, I was told, a book yet unfinished. It is still in the process of being written. I found myself looking back at all of my documented experiences. Every time I read something, I found another hidden message from years ago, a message to whose meaning I did not connect until now.

Those messages came into form. They became the book that I was meant to write. It took me twelve years of spiritual experiences to realize that God had planned this for me.

Isaac came forth again during an out-of-body experience on April 6, 2011:

Blessings, my children. I am Isaac. Believe in what you see. Believe in what you taste and hear. Believe in the sounds and the sights and every breath you take. Believe in every step you make. Divine energy and divine light is in all of the actions you take. Believe, just as God believes in all of you. Yet you ask, "Why should I believe?" You ask because you doubt what you see. You ask because you doubt what you hear, touch, feel, and smell. But your senses tell you it's real, and deep inside your soul you do believe. Believe and you will be fulfilled in so many ways. It is possible to see the truth. Just believe. Peace be with you all. I leave you now.

During one of my experiences, Archangel Michael and I walked side by side in heaven. He wanted to show me something. I looked at him in childlike anticipation, even asking what he wanted to show me. He smiled and asked me to be patient. We arrived at what I thought was the edge of a cliff top. "Keep walking," he said,

I took the next step forward, and found myself walking among the stars in the universe. I was totally awestruck by the sheer beauty and magnificence. Michael turned to me and said, "Beyond humanity's reach are other forms of life created by our Divine Lord."

"Why is it beyond our reach?" I asked.

"Because you are unable to reach yourselves and accept everything that God has created. You are not ready. Only when humanity embraces the truth will God give you the ability to see. It is then that the doors of the universe will be open to you." His words made so much sense to me.

We continued to walk. I noticed Michael smiling at me. "Each time you come home I have watched you," he said. "I can see that you do not want to return to the earthly plane."

"You are right. I do not want to return. Sometimes I feel selfish when I think that, for I have family whom I love very much and should not think of leaving them."

"It is not selfish. When you come here, you know you are home. You feel comforted here. You feel love. It is not strange to you."

I was happy that he understood. He continued, "Remember, the heart is the key of enlightenment. I know your heart and this is how I know everything about you. I know every soul created here by our Heavenly Father before they pass into the womb as a divine spark, and then are born as a child into the world. What lies ahead for you is to give these messages, to enlighten as many souls as you can. Awaken them. Speak to them. Tell them that our Divine Lord hears them. He feels them. So when you have reached them after you have revealed these revelations, they will begin to reach each other. This is what is expected of you. Help them see. Help them turn away from destroying what God made as perfection. Go forward my brother. We will forever continue to watch over you and all of God's creation."

My life and purpose make sense to me now. I have finally understood my gift and what is expected of me. So I must reach out to all. I cannot expect everyone to understand me and what I am trying to do, but I have hope. I have faith. If I can reach one person, it will feel like I have reached a thousand.

My guardian Isaac passed on to me a beautiful poem, which I would like to share with you:

To walk the road of despair.
I looked to my left
and I looked to my right
and I still saw despair.

How man has become so discontent.
How they look upon each other
and take and take.
They do not understand
the pain and despair they leave.
They just take and take.

So I continue to walk this road
and I begin not to despair
for I have hope and I see hope.
This hope begins to turn to faith
and this faith begins to turn to love,
and then I see at the end of this road
the light that is so clear
and that love and peace live there.

I am ready. My body is ready. My soul is ready to go wherever God takes me.

Words from the Divine

Each passing day as the sun rises and sets, as the moon rises and the stars shine, we look to the heavens and wish for miracles, wondering if God sees and hears His children. He does. Each star you see is the center of His eyes, looking upon His children, smiling. "No matter how much you weep, how much you speak, how much pain or suffering you have, I have never turned away from my children," he utters through our souls. "For as long as there is hope I will never leave you. My love for my children is endless and I will always forgive. For even those whom I will not forgive do not understand my power, my creation. Love and the heart is the key and for those who never see or feel this I still have love."

God looks for one glimmer, one true meaning and connection to Him. The faith and love carried in each heart produces the true connection. This is what God looks for always.

Epilogue

The last week of February 2016 proved difficult for Aycan and I. On Thursday, February 25, at 7.25 p.m., Aycan's cousin, who was very close to us, passed away a week after he fell into a coma. Up until a week before Guner passed away, he was a fit and healthy forty-three-year-old man. His passing came as a huge shock. For Aycan, it brought back all the feelings and emotions of losing her own brother, Behcet. He and Guner had grown up together and enjoyed a close bond.

That same night, Aycan and I were talking about what had happened when a huge surge of energy rushed through my body—followed by complete silence. The television was on and I could see Aycan coming toward me, but I couldn't hear a thing.

Within a split second, I was no longer in the room. Nothing new, but what made it unusual was that it had never happened within a few hours of somebody passing away. While being guided around heaven, my spiritual guide, Isaac, began to speak through me. Aycan wrote down what came from my mouth next, compliments of Isaac, at 11:08 p.m.:

> *Aycan, his suffering, his pain is over. He is being cleansed by your brother and then he shall walk beside his father. He has passed these words for you. He saw you standing from a distance. He thanks you for the support you gave his mother. He held your brother's hand. Your brother asked him three times if he was ready. In the end, he had no more to give. He wanted the pain to end. Do not weep, for it is beautiful here.*
>
> *As one light dims, another is lit. As one light dies, a brighter one is born. These lights, if you look up, are the stars, each one a soul watching over our earth. Each one a soul watching over humanity. Today, we welcome a beautiful light, and his light shall shine brightly among the others. You will see his light when you look up and you will know him. For he is now home where he begins his new beginning. Turn these tears to joy. Remember his life. He will never be forgotten. For when you look up to the stars, they are your loved ones looking over you all. I watch over you always.*

Aycan stopped dictating at 11:26 p.m.

Whenever I have such an experience, it takes me a while to completely come back to my body. Aycan tells me that it looks as though I am in a deep sleep from which I awaken slowly. My body temperature drops rapidly and I begin to shiver uncontrollably. Even though I am covered in a blanket, it takes a long time to feel like myself again.

On this night when I opened my eyes, Aycan quickly realized that I was not completely awake. She was right. I was only half here on earth, in my living room. The other half of me was still in heaven. There was something else I needed to share.

While Isaac spoke through me, I was given incredible insight to what happened to Guner's soul while he lay in a coma. The only way I can describe it is like a movie being played out in front of me, scene by scene. This had never happened to me before, not like this. I began speaking to Aycan in a low voice, my eyes half closed:

> *He was wrapped and then they laid him down. He was bathed with angels around him praying, almost singing. The water glistened, sparkling. You could call it holy water. His eyes were closed. It's very peaceful, very beautiful. One angel was speaking, giving words to him as he lay there, telling him he is now in the process of crossing over. They could sense the pulling of him going home, to God's garden. They were telling him his father is waiting once the cleansing is finished. He is wearing a pure white shroud, the energy shining bright from his chest; all the angels stood around him, pure white light. They said I was allowed to be there, as I was chosen to witness this. I asked, "Why are his eyes closed?"*

An angel replied, "He has to be completely cleansed before he can open his eyes. When he does open his eyes, he will be standing in the Creator's garden, heaven. His father will embrace him. They are all waiting. Not just family and friends, but everyone, for this is a celebration for them, welcoming home another brother." It's very hard to want to turn your back to how beautiful heaven is, but there are those who have seen heaven and have come back.

When Guner looked down at himself in the hospital, he could not understand what was going on and why everyone was working on him. Then he remembered hearing someone calling his name. He was looking everywhere while still in the room, trying to locate the voice. Then all of a sudden, he was no longer in the room. Only silence.

He opened his eyes and found himself in a field, looking left and right. Then he looked right behind him and saw your brother Behcet. Guner asked him, "Bro, what are you doing here?" and they hugged. He continued, "You look so young."

Your brother replied, "You don't look too bad yourself."

Guner then asked, "What do you mean?"

Behcet then showed Guner how young he looked. This was a place for them to meet so that Guner could understand what had happened to him. They were laughing, joking with each other. Then Guner said that *he was in a room looking down at himself. He said he remembered going to the hospital and that is all. He said he was floating around the room, where he could see people working on him, then he heard a voice calling him, and now here he is talking with Behcet. Behcet told him what had happened. Guner was upset but also curious. He was worried about his mother, children, and cousin, Aycan. Your brother told him he hadn't accepted what had happened because the voices of his family were calling him to wake up. He said to Behcet, "What do I do?"*

He replied, "There is a place here for you."

Guner then realized where he was. Behcet told him that he still had fight in him and he would not stand in the way of his fight. Guner said to Behcet, "If I let go, will they be okay?"

Behcet answered, "They will be fine. They will miss you as everyone misses their departed loved ones."

Guner was not sure. He felt their worry, sorrow, and frustration. He felt their panic. Behcet said, "It is a traumatic time for them. This is how it was for me." Guner asked Behcet if he still had a connection with his body. "You will until your confusion is over. It is the emotional tie you still feel with your body," Behcet explained.

Guner then said, "I do not feel any pain."

Behcet replied, "That is because your spirit has left your body. Even though you can see what they are doing to you, you cannot feel what they are doing, but you are still connected because of your heartbeat. Your heart will only stop beating when you have accepted what has happened. Do you want to go back? If you go back, you will not be the same person."

Guner returned back to his body just for a brief moment, to say goodbye to his loved ones. They thought he would pull through. That's why his eyes opened one last time. He did not want to leave so soon, like this. He felt there was more he had to do in his life, for his children. Even though he was a fighter, he just knew he couldn't beat this.

Finally, Aycan's cousin Guner left his body and walked into the light, where Behcet was waiting for him. They wrapped their arms around each other, smiling.

As painful as it was to hear these words, I also knew it would give Aycan and her cousin's family comfort to know that Guner was already with his loved ones, where his eternal life would continue . . .

About the Author

Senol Kiane was born in Hornsey, London, in 1961. Blessed with an ability that he did not fully embrace until the age of forty-one, he is a truly gifted individual. Not only is he a spiritual healer and spiritual motivational speaker, he also has a strong connection with the other side.

Wherever God Takes Me is a memoir documenting his life and out-of-body experiences and journeys, with a second memoir on the way. Senol has devoted his life to healing and helping those in need. He has given several inspirational talks in the UK and USA.

As well as being very connected to the universe spiritually, he is also interested in science fiction. He is a huge fan of Star Wars and collects Star Wars toys, or as he calls them, "collectibles." His favorite relaxing pastime is watching classic American comedies. Senol has 1,300 like-minded members in his Facebook group, Senol Kiane Into The Light, all of whom share inspiration and spirituality with each other.

Lightning Source UK Ltd.
Milton Keynes UK
UKHW010642190220
358976UK00001B/24